Frederick J Moss

Notes on Political Economy from the Colonial Point of View

Frederick J Moss

Notes on Political Economy from the Colonial Point of View

ISBN/EAN: 9783744645560

Printed in Europe, USA, Canada, Australia, Japan

Cover: Foto ©ninafisch / pixelio.de

More available books at **www.hansebooks.com**

NOTES

ON

POLITICAL ECONOMY

FROM THE COLONIAL POINT OF VIEW

BY

A NEW ZEALAND COLONIST

London

MACMILLAN AND CO., Limited

NEW YORK: THE MACMILLAN COMPANY

1897

All rights reserved

"The English shipowner it is plain" (from a certain Board of Trade paper) "finds it cheaper to hire foreign labour. In 1853 only 4·4 per cent of the crews were foreigners. The proportion has risen until in 1894 it was 16·95 per cent of the whole, not counting Lascars and Asiatics, who have increased until they are about one-eighth or one-ninth of the entire number. . . . The broad result is that in 1894 about two men did the work of seven on steam vessels in 1854, and that on sailing vessels two did the work of four. The decline has taken place chiefly among able seamen and apprentices."—The *Times*, 28th August 1895.

PREFACE

COLONISTS are continually warned that Capital is timid and easily frightened away. Yet the Capital thus personified is no airy material but a mass of the most solid substances—iron, coal, railways, roads, buildings, implements, machinery, ships, food and clothing, with a small proportion of gold and silver and the thousand other articles that enable man, by the labour of the present, to provide for the time to come. Excepting the gold and silver, they lie inert till credit touches them with its magic wand. Credit, not Capital, is the sensitive creation which so easily takes fright and hides away. To give a clear conception of the difference between the two is one of the objects which these notes have in view.

Again, neither the increase of Capital, nor of the national wealth of which it forms part, is the subject of difficulty in these days. The increase is sure. The problem is to make it sound and permanent by a reasonable partition of the annual product among the whole people. Any one honestly facing this question must be impressed with its complexity and with the momentous issues involved. The blunders and wrongdoing of ages have made it difficult to separate inequalities of human creation from those which Nature has imposed. To aid in some degree in unravelling the tangled skein is another of the objects which we have in view. To that end stress is laid on the several points—the pecuniary interests of the individual or the wider interests of the nation—from which economic questions may be regarded.

Geology and history alike tell the continuous development of man.

> "His way is down no fatal slope,
> But up to freer sun and air."

Each generation surpasses its predecessor in knowledge and in sympathy with its fellow-men. Each forms nobler conceptions of humanity, and the march is ever forward to some new goal. Every step not in accord with unmistakably existent public opinion is doomed to failure, and to prepare public opinion is the arduous work of the reformer. When this is accomplished the reforms fall naturally into place, and in that direction also these notes aim at being useful.

The extent and complexity of the economic problem may be illustrated by reference to the annual product of the industry of the United Kingdom. In the year 1889 that product was estimated as equivalent in coin to 1285 million of pounds sterling. Of the great mass of commodities thus represented, a portion equivalent to 1085 millions was consumed or used as Capital, leaving an estimated equivalent of 200 millions to form what are called the annual savings of the nation. Savings imply self-denial, which cannot be considered a characteristic of the greater capitalists to whom the 200 millions chiefly fell; and what they really represent is the surplus of production beyond the ordinary needs of the year. The problem of the age is to produce this vast mass of commodities without the terrible poverty at one end in contrast with the sickening superfluity at the other. Can this be done without changing the basis—the acquisitive instincts of man—on which material progress has hitherto rested? We believe that it can, and indulge the hope of casting some light in that direction also.

The State Socialist thinks otherwise. He proposes to reconstruct on a basis of altruism, and would make Governments the sole controllers of Capital and with it of the industry of nations. Can we hope, in the present stage of human development, to find a people sufficiently altruistic to create an altruistic government? To endow an ordinary human Government with the power now wielded by a number of competing Capitalists, in addition to the political power already in its hands, is a proposal not to be entertained by any who believe that power without efficient check is sure to end in gross abuse. Wherever such a check can be applied, the functions which are now taken up for personal gain might often be assumed by the Government with advantage to the nation. But the number of such functions is limited, and the conditions on which their assumption is possible will keep the limit within definite bounds.

The problems are complex and the difficulties great, but we cannot fold our hands and do nothing. The misery around and among us and the national safety forbid. The misery calls loudly for alleviation, and the alleviation must not cease till every man from whom the nation claims allegiance shall be saved, as of right, from risk of the degrading pauperism which he is now too often helpless to avert. Freedom of contract in the labour world will then become a reality, and a great step have been gained. Proper provision would also be made for that great mass of unemployed which the variation of the seasons and other unavoidable causes render indispensable as an industrial reserve.

Other reforms, especially in the occupancy of Land and in the control of the Currency will be needed, but every step will require to be deliberately weighed and taken with great care. There must be many grave differences, as to methods and means especially, before public opinion can be fairly settled and public acceptance of change secured. Political reforms have so far cleared the way that the field in every English-speaking country is open for the most full and free discussion of social and economical problems. In that direction also these notes are offered as a humble contribution from one who ventures to hope that much reading and a varied experience of man in different stages of civilisation may have enabled him to give them a title to consideration. The world is on the eve of great change. Knowledge is spreading. The discoveries of silver have deranged values, dislocated industrial society, and shaken nations to the core. The application of electricity as a motor is opening a new era in production as well as in transportation. Already, in the days of its early infancy, this motor is offered by the Niagara Company at the rate of seventy-two shillings per horse power for 365 days of twenty-four hours each. Is electricity, with its gigantic possibilities, to follow the course of steam, to become a gatherer of superfluous wealth for the few, and give to the mass a still narrower choice between incessant and bitter strife or submission to practical slavery? The answer is still in our hands. As the twig is bent so will the tree incline.

CONTENTS

CHAPTER I

INDIVIDUALISM: ITS RISE AND FALL

Definition of Political Economy—The earlier Economists—The Nation subordinated to the Man—Law of Rent—Wages Fund—Law of Population—Efforts at more suitable partition — Doctrines of extreme individualism — Later Economists—Growth of the New School—Human nature the primary element — Earlier stages of social development — Absence of stimulus to individual exertion — Tribal trading — Substitution of Money for barter — Gold and Silver as money — New era with Gold and Silver — The ideal society — Effects of wider education —The patriotic leader . . . Pages 1 to 33

CHAPTER II

THE NATION AND NATIONALISM

What is a Nation?—The Nation a living organism—Individualism and Nationalism—Patriotism and its growth—

Patriotism in the British Colonies — The Protectionist Policy of Colonies—Evolution of a National Spirit—Later Economists take man in all aspects — National Wealth must grow concurrently with a healthy National Life — Hardship and privation unavoidable, and neither injurious nor degrading—Much may be entrusted to a properly organised State—Wealth cannot be too great in a Nation —No single panacea possible—Yearly production enough for the needs of all, with vast amount to spare—What will the coming century have to tell? . Pages 34 to 62

CHAPTER III

NATIONAL WEALTH

Definition of National Wealth — Definition of Individual Wealth—To be Wealth, must embody human labour— Soil, Sea, and Rivers the only trustworthy and enduring sources of National Wealth—Sources of Wealth and Capital—Wealth of the United Kingdom—National liabilities in United Kingdom and in Colonies contrasted — Other evils of too rapid expenditure of borrowed Capital—Some investments of Capital by the United Kingdom—Misleading use of terms, and the great functions of Credit in exchange—Vital importance of the small amount of Specie —Panic if Specie fall below a certain point—Influence of National Debts in creating a private control over Credit circulation . . . . Pages 63 to 87

CHAPTER IV

The Creation of National Wealth

Conditions for creating National Wealth—Transportation and Fiscal Protection—East India Company as a Monopoly—New Zealand Company—Breaking up of tribal organisation and tribal rights to land — Original land tenure in New Zealand—A landless people entirely dependent on money—Beginning of wage dependence—The old English Guilds—Objects to be kept in view—Five centuries of struggle—Power of Labour aided by Capital—National Capital indispensable; its preservation the first consideration—The worst enemies of progress and society—The old political issues played out . . Pages 88 to 111

CHAPTER V

Capital and Credit

Definition of Capital—Origin of Capital—Power of machinery in production — Machinery displacing human labour — Labour becoming more dependent on Capital—Small proportion of labour in cost of production—Machinery power of the United Kingdom — Crystallisation into present extremes of rich and poor—Commercial Credit Paper, its character and functions—Landed Credit—Financial Credit the master of all—Recent operations of a Syndicate with the United States Treasury—Agreement with the Syndicate—Treasury compelled to put itself under the Syndicate's wing—State must recover control of the Currency—Inequality of sacrifice in present taxation—A Nation must be its own master—The new motive power. Shall it be the servant or the master of the people? Pages 112 to 142

CHAPTER VI

Joint-Stock Companies

Power of Joint-Stock Companies: their principles and practice: their present position—Denounced in 1655—Their power becoming a public danger—Company Capital and Bank Capital—The Bank of England: its origin—Opening of the Bank of England and Joint-Stock Banks—Present position of Bank of England—Present position of Joint-Stock Banks—Foreign and private Banks in United Kingdom—The growth of the National Debt—Rates at which National Debt incurred — Modern Monarchs of Finance .   .   .   .   . Pages 143 to 165

CHAPTER VII

Value and Price

Value, Price, and the Precious Metals as commodities and measures of value—Illustrations of Value and Price—Natural Price and Market Price—Market Price considered—Costs of production—Labour Power and Wages—The

Living Wage—Respective positions of Capital and Labour in production—Industries unable to pay a Living Wage are a public nuisance—Industrial leaders to be paid suitably but kept in check—Effect of abundance or scarcity of precious metals on price—The Demonetisation of Silver—Varying effects of Appreciation and Depreciation in different countries—Effect on communities with large wage dependent classes—A Living Wage the first claim on all production . . . . Pages 166 to 192

CHAPTER VIII

Exchange

Mutual benefit in Exchange—Domestic and Foreign Trade—Functions of Foreign Trade—Export Trade in Colonies—Imports exceeding Exports—Exports exceeding Imports—What we may hope—General Booth in Sydney
Pages 193 to 204

CHAPTER I

INDIVIDUALISM—ITS RISE AND FALL

MANY definitions of political economy have been given. For our purpose it may be defined as a term to indicate the investigation of phenomena connected with the creation of national wealth and with its subsequent partition among the people. The use of the term national implies that each nation is the subject of separate inquiry, and that results are to be measured by their effect on that particular nation and not on the world at large.

<small>Purposes of political economy.</small>

At the outset we have to note an important difference between the creation and the partition of a nation's wealth. The creation is a natural evolution incident to the possession of hands and brain and to the necessity of making provision for the morrow. Its progress depends upon the character of the people, the stability of their political arrangements, the security for their lives and property, and the resources at their command. On the other hand, the partition depends almost entirely on human laws and customs which vary from time to time among all nations. Improvements in production, transport, and distribution are potent in the creation of wealth. They are still more potent in its partition when the means of improvement are legalised as private property without attempt at some concurrent check on the passion for gain to which they offer constantly increasing opportunity and temptation.

The earlier Economists were occupied chiefly with inquiries into the creation of wealth. They did great service in exposing the mischief done by worn-out monopolies and other obstacles to free action and free exchange among a people bearing common burdens, living under common responsibilities, and possessing a common administration. They exposed the fallacy of regarding the gain of coin as the end of foreign commerce, and of regarding the precious metals as the most valuable of a nation's acquisitions. They reduced to a system investigations previously confused and vague, but unfortunately aimed at

The earlier Economists.

making political economy an exact science. For this purpose it was assumed, as a self-evident axiom, that an innate desire for pecuniary gain was the universal stimulus to individual exertion and the origin of wealth to the nation. The accumulations of individuals formed the national wealth. The portions which some were pleased to abstain from consuming and devote to new production, formed the Capital of the nation.

The nation subordinated to the man.

This theory subordinated the nation to the man. His fellow-countrymen were taught that they owed to him, to his superior natural endowments and to his virtuous self-denial, the opportunity of earning their own subsistence and of helping to maintain the strength and progress of the nation. The capitalist was exalted and the worker lowered in pro-

INDIVIDUALISM: ITS RISE AND FALL 5

portion, while the highest statesmanship was held to consist in leaving to each wealth-seeker the widest field with the least possible restriction. The effect of his enterprise on the well-being of others and upon the physical and moral health of the nation, was a matter with which governments had small concern. Every one best understood his own interests and should be left to pursue them with the least possible interference. This was the natural, simple, and true way of advancing the interests of the nation.

A law of rent was devised and made to declare, as an edict of Nature, that the amount paid for rent represented only the natural advantages of one piece of land over the worst which was found worth occupation at the time.

Law of rent.

Wages fund. A definite wages fund was discovered, and the remuneration of labour declared to be absolutely dependent on the amount of that fund and the number of labourers among whom it was to be divided. Wages were thus a simple question of demand and supply, with the demand unalterably fixed and the supply a varying but ever redundant quantity. It followed that rent and wages were regulated by natural laws, and that any attempt to lower the one or to raise the other by combination, or by any other means, was a contest with Nature and doomed to failure.

Law of population. Last, but far from least, came the law of population, which declared that masses of men, of women, and of children, had been always doomed by their Creator to want and misery because food could only be increased in arithmetical gradation while human beings multiplied in a geometrical ratio. Man was continually outgrowing the capacity of Mother Earth to sustain him, and must struggle on against an elastic but ever-increasing pressure from which escape was impossible. Here was a crowning discovery. The aids to be obtained from science and invention were quietly ignored, while they who had acquired personal wealth were freed from responsibility for the misery around them. No wonder that the creed became popular among the rich and powerful, and that the comforting science of political economy evoked their admiration and received generous support.

Amid the chorus of gratulation which followed this discovery, the voice of the <small>Efforts at a more suitable partition.</small>

unbeliever had small chance of being heard. Efforts were made by a few to obtain a more suitable partition of the yearly national product, but such efforts were denounced as ignorant presumption. The poor were benevolently accepted as a creation of the Almighty, for has He not said, " the poor ye have always with you." Man could only give aid so that they might not perish by absolute starvation. At the same time, for their own sakes and for the interests of society, the aid when accepted must entail a certain degree of ignominy in order that unworthy claimants (for whom ignominy has no terrors) might be kept within due bounds. When evil and misery grew unbearable and the sufferers dared to rebel, the Statute law, the State forces, and Starvation were always at hand to vindicate economical science and to teach a salutary economical lesson.

On these foundations were built the doctrines of extreme individualism, held to contain the only creed worthy of enlightened men or adapted to make a progressive nation. To accumulate material wealth was the great end of men and nations. He who succeeded was the fittest to survive. His survival did not imply their entire extinction, but a continued life of helpless misery for masses of his fellow-countrymen. He had what was called a stake in the country and a right to every political privilege. He who did not succeed, from whatever cause it might be, was unworthy of political rights or of voice in the affairs of a country in whose defence his life was to be given, whose laws affected his daily existence and

Doctrines of extreme individualism.

to fill whose ranks he reared recruits with lifelong sacrifice. Property was everything and man merely an element in its creation. The creed took well with those who controlled affairs, and its preachers were welcomed as masters in the great science of political economy. Its terrible pressure on masses of the people may be read in the story of the life and labours of the Earl of Shaftesbury about the middle of this century. There we see the cruel suffering endured by thousands of helpless women and children as well as by grown men. There we see how bitterly Lord Shaftesbury's mischievous meddling was denounced by the great money gatherers of the time, how they resented his wicked attacks on the freedom of contract and the personal liberty sacredly dear to all true Englishmen, and how darkly they pictured the ruin which he was working to the manufacturing and the commercial prosperity on which depended the safety and greatness of the nation. Lord Shaftesbury nobly persevered. He did much, but how much remains to be done we see by the reports of Parliamentary Committees, of Royal Commissions, and of other trustworthy investigators, to the present day.

Later Economists have taken a wider view. First among them we must rank John Stuart Mill, whose mind, though saturated with the old economy, was so clear, honest, and strong as to carry him to the borderland and give glimpses of fairer fields beyond. His review of Thornton's work on the claims of labour was a sign of the coming change. This review appeared in the *Fortnightly* in

The later Economists.

May 1869. Till then, all "good, sound, and scientific Economists"—including Mill —held that attempts to raise individual wages must end in failure. The laws of supply and demand and the fixed limit of the wages fund were irresistible. Mill gallantly admitted that Thornton had the best of the argument, and he had himself come to the conclusion that Trade Unions, judiciously guided, might obtain an increase in individual wages without reduction in the number of workers. Here began the fall of the wages fund. Other myths were speedily attacked, and among them that of supply and demand as regulating the price of commodities. It was proved that the reverse held good, that price regulated both demand and supply, and only ceased its fluctuations when they were brought to an equilibrium. These and other myths fell, but Malthus's great discovery of the law of population, modified into a tendency instead of an absolute law, has its narrowed circle of believers at the present day.

The new School has grown rapidly in influence and in numbers. Its followers have thrown off much that the old School held dear, and even questioned the possibility of building an exact science on a factor so variable as man. They quickly noted that the greatest personal accumulations have been made by devices which drew the earnings of a multitude into the pockets of one, without the transfer adding an iota to the wealth of the nation. They noted how great had often been the power of custom, of public opinion, and of the

Growth of the new School.

higher and nobler feelings in regulating the occupation of land, the partition of the general wealth, and the economical relations of men. They saw that the amount of rent was not dictated by any natural law, but was consequent on the human laws which made land a marketable and necessarily a more or less monopolised commodity. They noted especially that labour was not to be ranked with ordinary commodities, and was not subject to their conditions. Even in the bargaining for labour the practice was exceptional, in that the price was initiated by the buyer and not by the seller in each transaction. They boldly denounced the cheapness which was regarded by the old School as a decisive test; and declared it to be a national injury when obtained at the cost of misery and degradation to their fellow-countrymen. They held that the creation of wealth was a means and not an end—a means of adding to the strength of the nation and to the enjoyment, health, and progress of its people. They refused to confine their researches to the operation of the sordid side of human nature, and held the partition of the nation's wealth to be a subject exceeding all others in importance because concentration was capable of making wealth a curse instead of a blessing to the nation. Finally they discarded the methods of deduction from assumed premises, and substituted induction from facts carefully gathered and from wide historical investigation.

In the new Economy, human nature in all its fulness became the first element to be *Human nature the primary element.*

taken into account, and human nature has ever been the same. Men are to-day in their instincts just what they were when the earliest Pharaohs ruled in Egypt, when the fleets of Carthage traversed every known sea, when heathen Vykings ravaged their neighbours' coasts, and when the descendants of those Vykings landed on Plymouth rock to found in peace a new free nation. The violence may be modified or the direction of these instincts may be changed, but they remain. We see in constant operation the selfish faculties necessary to preserve the individual. We see also the altruistic qualities from which spring the higher aspirations necessary for the progress of the race and the preservation of the family, the tribe, or the nation. The growth of altruism appears remarkably coincident with a development of the nervous system, which forms the chief physical distinction between the savage and the civilised man. This development is manifested in increased mental activity, bodily restlessness, sensitiveness to noise and similar external disturbances, but above all in readier sympathy with suffering and distress. Where the civilised man pities, the savage sees only ground for mockery and sport. So marked is the change that some have feared the growth becoming morbid and weakening the hardihood on which the existence of a nation, as well as its commercial enterprise, must depend. There can be little ground for fear on this head so long as physical labour continues to be a chief condition of national life. Meanwhile we may safely regard altruism as a product of civilisation, unknown among savage races and little known among those even well removed from actual barbarism.

Earlier stages of social development.   In the earlier stages of corporate existence the family is the unit of the community and includes numerous adopted children who, with their descendants, enjoy the rights and are subject to the obligations of blood relations. A number of families tracing descent from a common ancestor form the tribe in which is vested the supreme ownership of land, the control of the relation of the respective families to the tribe, and of the tribe's relation to outsiders. The usufruct of the land is with the particular family whose right is recognised by the tribe, and again with the member or members of that family whose right is recognised by the family Head. Within each family the will of its Head is law, but the exercise of that will is subject to customs which generally have a religious sanction and which regulate every concern of daily life. Every tribe, however deficient in morality in our sense of the word, has its code of honour, and every member has an almost morbid fear of doing anything which, according to that code, would not be right.

The demands of the code and of tribal custom are imperative, and among them is the duty of sharing food and shelter with all kinsmen in need. With wider intercourse new commodities are introduced. The old obligation is extended to them, and a system of reciprocal give and take becomes the method of putting movable property into circulation. This is not communism

The tribal code.

though often mistaken for it by the casual observer. The ownership is with the possessor, but subject to regulation by public opinion, a power which no uncivilised man will ever dream of disregarding.

<small>Absence of stimulus to individual exertion.</small>

Under such conditions the stimulus to individual exertion is reduced to a minimum. Every one has land to occupy. The sick, the widow, the orphan, and the weak are assured of a home however rude; while a certain uniformity in mode of life brings all, from the highest chief to the lowest slave, in touch with one another. Movable property is small and land is the only possession of great value. Land means retainers and power, and men will fight, rob, cheat, and strive for land as eagerly as they do for valued possessions in more advanced communities. The difference is that in the one case the land is prized for the number of stalwart men and healthy women and children whom it will support. In the other, the land is prized for the pleasure or pecuniary gain which it may bring to the owner without regard to any other consideration.

Time contracts are unknown in the early stage of corporate growth. For abstract or complex ideas, the language of a savage race has no terms of expression. All transactions are direct and by barter. An authoritative declaration of tribal custom settles every dispute. The dealings are between tribe and tribe through representatives selected by each. The subsequent partition among families rests with the chief, and among the members of such families it rests with the family Head. *Tribal trading.*

Trade between individuals of a tribe is of very much later growth, and comes with the introduction of new articles giving birth to new desires and requiring greater labour to obtain the means for their gratification. The advent of strangers gives also undreamed of value to articles, pearl shell and sandal wood for example, which have long lain waste. They now become eagerly desired and lead even to fighting for their acquisition. Slowly but steadily individual interests grow, and one of the earliest manifestations would probably be the taking of payment, from members of his own tribe, by some wizard claiming the power of miraculous cure or other occult means of service.

Substitution of money for barter.   The advent of strangers from distant lands is the first great stimulator of trade and production among savage races. As exchanges increase, some single commodity is adopted to express exchangeable values and to be a substitute, by delivery, for one of the two articles handled in all ordinary barter. This commodity is called money, and has at various times consisted of various objects,—of tobacco, for example, among the early colonists of Virginia; of cowrie shells among the negroes of Western Africa; and of gold and silver or legally authorised issues of paper among modern nations. To rank as money a commodity must possess both characteristics. It must be of universal acceptance by delivery in payment of obligations, and express the exchangeable ratios of commodities with each other, which ratios we call their price. In the Fijian islands a whale's tooth was the most precious of all commodities and had the most commanding power in exchange. But the whale's tooth was never used as a definite expression of price, and could not be ranked as money. It was, like the diamond among ourselves, a commodity pure and simple, and formed no part of the currency of the country.

Gold and silver as money.

Gold and silver soon beat all other substances, as money, out of the field. Embodying human labour in their production, they were marketable commodities. Being by nature durable, divisible, and portable, they are eminently suited to be stamped as coin. Credit did not begin to play its more delicate, more complex, and infinitely more extensive part in exchange, until a higher stage with great facilities of communication had been reached.

A new era began with the adoption of *New era with gold and* the precious metals as money. Operations *silver.* in distant markets became easier, and a new stimulus was given to production. Commerce increased, and its spirit, essentially selfish, gave a new tone to social and industrial life. Business has no room for sentiment or for any feeling which might interfere with pecuniary gain. The old tribal and family obligations became burdensome as wants increased, and they were gradually narrowed to suit the times. Their tradition long remained. The poor relation continued to receive a cordial welcome to his kinsman's home. Trading between relations was distasteful, and scarcely less so between friends. To take interest for money lent to any person was stigmatised as usury, but for money lent to relations or friends was regarded as meanness unspeakable. To keep open house for wayfarers was a sacred duty, but all customs wax feeble and disappear with change in the conditions of life to which they were originally due. To-day the Christmas family gathering is perhaps the only survival and shadowy reminder of a vanished time.

<small>Beginnings of individual self-dependence.</small> With the disappearance of the system of general give and take, came a condition in which every man must depend on his own exertions to make provision for present and prospective needs. Hereby a new, worthy, and powerful incitement to exertion was created, an incitement still animating the tiller of the soil, the fisher of the sea, the worker in the mine, and the millions whose labour, often at the peril of their lives, is

indispensable to the creation of a nation's wealth and to the equally necessary work of transport and distribution. Men will be prompted, till the long-looked-for millennium, to exploit for their own personal gain the labour of their fellow-men. The so-called struggle for existence is not, as the term would imply, a struggle with natural enemies or for life, but a sordid, brutal fight of man with man for supremacy and rule. The energy of a few is intensified by this struggle, but the desire of all men to make provision for themselves and for those whom they hold most dear, has been and ever must be the solid stimulus to individual industry and the root of wealth to the nation.

The ideal society would be that in which all have the opportunity to satisfy this worthy desire by a reasonable amount of

The ideal society.

labour whether mental or manual. The perfect attainment of this ideal is impracticable in our present state of civilisation. None the less is it well to keep the ideal in mind and to seek its attainment, step by step, as the conditions of life and the state of public opinion may permit. Much has been gained in the past. None can doubt that more will be gained as knowledge spreads, and as men's minds become impressed with the insignificance of the individual in face of the grandeur of the nation to whose labour and protecting care he owes all that makes life worth living.

Effect of wider education.

The general spread of education cannot fail to be powerful in this direction. The passage from the old condition to the new, with education only half completed, will doubtless be a time of trouble. But that will pass with fuller enlightenment and with the respect for others' rights and feelings which enlightenment brings. Higher and nobler views of life will prevail, tastes be improved and intercourse between men of all conditions be made easier and more agreeable. Wealth will lose much of the public consideration which tends to create an inordinate desire for its possession, and we can imagine a time when men will speak as apologetically of their great wealth as they often already do, in the Colonies, of their great landed possessions. The divorce between the political and the social worlds is daily becoming more pronounced in all free countries, and with it the threatened rule of a mere plutocracy will fade away. In the Colonies a commercial aristocracy, with no other idea of government than one based on commercial principles, has always stood face to face with the wage dependents and none over or between them. Sixteen thousand miles of ocean separating the Colonies from the great centres of commerce and population in the older world, gave to the wage dependents an advantage which they were not slow to turn to account. Free education and free government were called to their aid, and we see them now indignantly repelling the principle that interests are to rule and men to be a secondary consideration,—the principle by which plutocracy is guided and on which its ideas of government are based. Nor is an educated people likely to accept the ideal of the individualist who regards the transformation of a nation into an opulent bank, a huge workshop or a noisy exchange mart for other nations, as the highest progress and civilisation.

To render his own country an abiding home for his own countrymen will be the aim of the true leader of an educated and a patriotic people. Their universal prosperity and purchasing power, and not the purchasing power of foreigners, will be his foremost dependence. Their wages, their hours of labour, and their welfare, will not be regulated by the standards of life in competing and less civilised communities. None will heed the arguments of selfish, wealth-worshipping cliques, in whose creed no place is left for the personal independence and lofty spirit without which permanent national existence becomes impossible. *The patriotic leader.*

Anticipations of this nature have passed beyond the region of dreams. Their gradual attainment is clearly possible. The inertia natural to man, and the aversion to change natural to nations having a large proportion of older people of fixed ideas and habits, as well as the great vested interests concerned, have to be taken into account. But none of these obstacles is insuperable, and we may confidently hope that the progress of the past will be continued until mankind are relieved from all the preventable miseries under which they have so long and so grievously suffered.

No more happy augury could be desired than the downfall of the narrow doctrines of individualism. Backed by their queer connection with an ideal reign of universal peace based on business interests, these doctrines almost sanctified personal selfishness in its hardest and meanest forms; in the government and in the policy of nations. There could be little hope of real progress for mankind at large while this wretched creed blocked the way.

CHAPTER II

NATIONALISM

What is a nation? THE nation was regarded by the older Economists as an association of individuals for the preservation of internal law and order and for defence against external foes. The government was chief of police and guardian of the public safety. The more closely it confined itself to these duties the better the government and the more prosperous the people. A poor conception of the position and duties of a government, but infinitely more poor of the union of hearts as well as of interests which constitutes a nation,—a union capable of exciting the glow of patriotism,—a union for which mothers proudly send their sons to battle, and for which the sons proudly die. We might as reasonably look upon the man himself as a mere collection of living atoms, and take no note of the hidden spirit which gives new life, new powers, and a new character to the whole. This subtle spirit is to be found in every crowded assemblage of human beings, carrying away the most cold blooded, causing him to lose his personal identity and to become absorbed in the mass around him.

The nation, like the man, is a living organism having an existence connected with yet distinct from that of the individual atoms of which it is composed. Men die and their places know them no more, but

The nation a living organism.

the nation lives for ever. The preservation of the national life in health and vigour is the paramount object of political economy. The wealth of the individual is only of account so far as it aids in attaining this object. If the wealth has a contrary tendency it stands self-condemned.

The individualist and the nationalist.

These two widely different views as to what constitutes a nation lead to grave practical results. The individualist creed is based upon the one. The creed of his opponent, usually called Socialist, but for whom Nationalist would be the more appropriate term, is based upon the other. To the Individualist the man and his personal interests are the primary element.

To the Nationalist the nation is the supreme consideration, and the man only an atom soon to yield his place to a successor. The Nationalist eliminates from economical questions all distinction between classes, interests, industries, or men. In his view any system or industry which entails misery and degradation upon the many, however gainful to a few, saps the national vitality and is a nuisance calling for removal. He adheres to the old simple rule of judging the tree by its fruit, and that fruit is the health and strength of the nation. This is his supreme test involving the assumption that the duty of the State—represented by the Government—is not confined to military and police, but includes all practicable means for defending its weaker members against destructive aggression from their stronger fellow-countrymen, let the aggression take what form it may.

Patriotism and its growth.

Patriotism is the force by which the national life is maintained, and patriotism cannot exist without a sense of living nationality which is always of slow and painful growth. We may follow its development most readily among communities formed in modern historical times by emigration from peoples in an advanced stage of civilisation. To this day, for example, in the greatest of these modern offshoots, the United States of America, it is a moot question when the spirit of nationality first assumed a dominant influence among them. Was it at the Declaration of Independence or at the adoption of the Federal Constitution ? Was it after the second war with England or after their great Civil War ? These are questions still debated among American writers who are united only on the one point—that the dependent colonial spirit coloured their life and gave a tone to their politics long after independence had been asserted and won. Closer and better opportunities of observation are offered by the great existing British Colonies endowed with the most ample powers of self-government, and independent in all but the name.

Watching the progress of these Colonies, we note the rapid growth of local attachments and rivalries which seem only the tribal feeling in a new form; but we note also that patriotism is reserved entirely for the nation from which they sprung. Its flag is their flag. Its customs and opinions are their guide. Even its prejudices and animosities are incorporated in their politics and their life. Meanwhile the altered conditions of existence in a

_{Patriotism in the British Colonies.}

new land silently work changes of a far-reaching kind. These communities began their career with ideas and needs which could only be satisfied by joint action. Very quickly they learned to use the State's credit and the State's financial resources for the common good. They used them to provide roads, railways, telegraphs, water-works, gas-works, tramways, docks, and numerous other accessories to make their new land more productive and their new home more habitable. They used the State to build schools and colleges, and to give a free education to the people. They used it for many similar purposes, and still carry its action into fields which are held, in the older land, sacred to exploitation by private persons for private gain. They know that this employment of State action is not without drawbacks. Nothing human can be, but colonists place against them the great and evident gain to the community. In the consequent diffusion of comfort and in the spirit of independence and self-respect among all ranks of the people, they see ample reply and justification. Abuses rise, but colonists regard the mischief as merely passing, while the good achieved is permanent and not to be gainsaid.

An even more marked deviation from the creed of the Individualist is quickly seen. The British colonist is scarcely seated in the saddle when he begins a furious tilt against one of its most cherished articles. He discards all theories of free trade with the outer world and levies high import duties on every product which *The protectionist policy of British Colonies.*

his colony is capable of supplying in adequate quantity for its own needs. He levies these duties even on the products of the country under whose flag he lives. He believes that only in this way can his new land be made a prosperous field for emigration from the old, and that prosperity so large as this aim implies will not be attainable while subject to unrestricted competition with the great Capital, the power of giving unlimited credit, and the more poorly paid labour of older lands. Their surplus stocks are dumped upon his own market to be sold at any price in order to prevent a fall in the far greater quantity which the exporter sells at home. When the colonist is told that to obtain these goods so cheaply is a boon, he refuses to recognise the right of any man to receive such boons at the cost of suffering to his own people.

In addition to these incentives to a policy of protection, the colonist desires that the children growing up around him may have opportunities of acquiring mechanical skill, and so saved from becoming mere hewers of wood and drawers of water for richer nations. He regards mechanical skill and the great products of that skill as the buttress of a people's strength and safety. He is firmly convinced that without a variety in industries no single industry can thrive, and that without a local ready market for a variety of agricultural products the proper rural settlement of his new country is impossible. These are the considerations which make nearly every British colonist, who is not a trader in imported commodities, strongly protectionist in policy. He does not regard immediate results. His eye is on the future and on the children growing up around him. The great risk, in his view, is that protection may make fortunes for a few employers while doing little for the employed. To this he is fully alive, but trusts to widespread education and to perfect freedom for arming alike the people of all classes and enabling them to find a suitable remedy when the need for such remedy shall come. Let what may happen his new policy is full of hope, and is strengthened by the conviction that it cannot breed more harm or be more injurious, under any circumstances, than the individualist form of free trade which it has replaced.

Such are the ideas and such the motives at the bottom of this unorthodox and apparently unpatriotic policy which the British Colonies so universally adopt. There is not the faintest tinge of unpatriotic feeling in it all, but they who look below the surface must see the force of the undercurrent which is thus set in motion. They see in these protectionist proclivities the first thin rift between the Fatherland and those lands which are being built up, under its flag and protection, as future homes for a redundant population, and as new fountains of life for the British race, which has already made the English tongue dominant among the languages of the world.

We see in these self-governing colonies, still without the least consciousness of a national feeling of their own, how slowly

The first small rift.

Evolution of a national spirit.

and with what difficulty the national spirit is evolved. History, tradition, language, literature, intercourse, modes of thought and habits of life, long counteract the centrifugal tendency even where men of different nations but kindred races are introduced into the new community. Absolute freedom and self-government have left the greater of the British Colonies without direct grievance of any kind, and the connection with the Fatherland is cherished by generations of whom few have ever wandered from the land of their own birth. It would be idle, for all that, to overlook the influence exerted by pride of growth, by new surroundings, and by new views of life. Already there is exhibited a vague feeling of discontent with their hybrid position, and nothing grates more harshly on the colonial ear than the frequent coupling them with India "and our other possessions." They are denied the right to use the national flag, and do not form integral parts of the Empire. Their self-respect is in this way often wounded, and so doubtless was that of the old North American Colonies, who went through all these little shocks with many great and solid material grievances to boot. Yet we know that their loyalty to the Fatherland was hard to shake, and that it endured till human nature could no longer bear the strain. Then came the final shock which stirred the smouldering embers into flame, welded the disjointed mass into solid union, and put into it a living soul. Through trials and troubles a new nation, centre of new hopes and new aspirations, was born among men. A new flag was seen, and for the honour of that flag men were as ready to die as their fathers were for the honour of the old. Gradually the colonial feeling gave way, but even with a separate flag, years passed before a distinctive American national spirit took firm hold of the new people. How can we regard a nation so born and so matured as a mere joint-stock association? How regard it as other than a divine creation and an organism as distinct as man?

Later Economists take man in all his aspects.   The older Economists would regard considerations of this nature as irrelevant to what they were pleased to call their science. The newer Economists think differently. They take man in all his varied aspects. Families form tribes, and tribes grow into a nation. The growth is an evolution, and each stage has its own economic as well as ethical conditions. Each is distinct from the other, as distinct as the death-dirge of a savage chief or the war-whoop of a savage tribe from the anthem of a nation or the hymn of the Marscillaise. From the day of its birth the nation embodies all that men hold most dear. It is all in all. The man, however great in intellect or high in character, is but one of the ever-changing myriads of which it is composed. He will vanish and his place be taken by another to continue the work from the point at which he left it. Poor indeed is the people and desperate its condition when such replacement cannot be promptly made.

The great necessity for the acquisition of national wealth is admitted as fully by the nationalist as by the most extreme teachers of the individualist school. He is not of

National wealth must grow concurrently with a healthy national life.

those who decry its possession, for he believes that without wealth national progress is impossible. But his efforts are directed to make progress concurrent with a healthy and vigorous national life, which cannot be attained without the physical and mental development of the whole people. He would bring out in each whatever of mind and manhood may be lying dormant within him. The free education fast becoming the birthright of every English-speaking child throughout the world, is a recognition of this principle. The time must come when a similar recognition will be extended to the right of a decent subsistence for these children when young, and of opportunity to earn that subsistence when the days of education are past. Personal destitution, ruinous and demoralising, but too often now unavoidable, will then be rarely seen, and confirmed pauperism, the canker of civilisation, will be unknown. Ample field would still be left for the individual exertion of energetic men. To preserve such a field is a national necessity. Men are created with unequal powers, varying tastes, and widely different desires. The struggle to which these lead is necessary for the development of the race, but that struggle must not and need not demand a life's deadening toil for often less than a bare and brutish subsistence.

Under the most favourable conditions which reason can forecast, hardship and privation will always be found. But hardship and privation are not degrading. Nor are they inconsistent with happiness so long as health, pure air and hope, with the

Hardship and privation unavoidable and neither injurious nor degrading.

simplest food and shelter, go with them. Bellamy's people, shielded perpetually from wind and weather, and able to command music or a church service while lying lazily in bed, would not be happier, and certainly would be feebler, than less pampered mortals. The foul air that saps health and deadens the soul, and the hopelessness that breeds despair, are the worst enemies of civilised man. To combat them, to see that all may have pure air, and to instil hope into all breasts, will be the highest point which statesmanship can attain. They are the modern equivalent of the fowl in every peasant's pot which the noblest of French kings aimed at as a crowning glory, but which the assassin's knife left a dream.

With political arrangements to decentralise administration and to distribute power, with a vigilant people suitably educated, and with perfect publicity in public affairs, much might be entrusted to the State without perilling public freedom or unduly limiting the field for individual energy. Above all, the most complete publicity must be insisted upon in State transactions. Public bodies working under this condition would be safer in every sense than joint-stock companies working secretly, exercising great secret political influence, and without effective supervision till bankruptcy casts upon them the bull's-eye of the law, showing too often the public corruption they have fostered and the private ruin they have wrought. Undertakings in which secrecy is held necessary are unfit to be touched by the

Much may be entrusted to a properly organised State.

State. They are almost invariably designed to take advantage of weakness, credulity, or ignorance in order to obtain personal gain. The State, bound to protect all equally, can have nothing to do with them.

Wealth a benefit, and cannot be too great in a nation.

No nation was ever yet too rich, though many have fallen by undue concentration of their wealth, and by undue concentration of the land from which that wealth is primarily obtained. Rome fell amid unparalleled splendour, because her wealth was confined to the few, and she could not, in the hour of need, find adequate defenders among her millions of landless and poverty-stricken people. Across the page of history we see Oriental nations flitting with bejewelled princes who have left a record of gorgeous palaces and the ruins of magnificent monuments, all extorted from the enforced toil of a spiritless, degraded, and helpless people. Spain, whose nobles and whose churches were gorged with the rich plunder of a newfound world, fell rapidly from her great estate, while the buccaneers who robbed her galleons and ravaged her colonial coasts scattered widely their plunder and ministered to the growth of more free and more industrious nations. In this light it is a happy reflection that modern nations depend upon work and not upon plunder for the wealth on which their civilisation is built. To wealth we owe the means of easy intercourse, of exchanging ideas, of enlarging and storing knowledge, of subduing the forces of nature to the use of man, and of securing the greatest of all earthly blessings the independence of the nation.

<small>No single panacea possible.</small>
Evil comes not from wealth, but from the abuses which lead to disastrous inequality in its distribution, and which plunge multitudes into misery and degradation while leaving the few to revel in a superabundance quite as demoralising from the national point of view. No single panacea is possible, and the search for one can only lead to waste of time and energy. The ills to be remedied have their roots in abuse of human weakness and of human ignorance. Weakness we shall always have, and reform, to be effective, must be many-sided. Each evil must be traced to its source, and public opinion brought to bear upon it with full effect. When the fitting time has come, the remedy will be applied

without the arbitrary and inquisitorial legislation in which panacea promoters find delight. Take the persistent attempts of the Prohibitionist to override the tastes of millions and to force them into his mould by sheer compulsion. If he succeeded, would the causes of drunkenness be eradicated, and wherein would a people so constrained be raised in personal manliness or national life? How vain too is the panacea of universal thrift so loudly urged as the saviour of nations. In the sense of not wasting any of the gifts of God, thrift is a duty incumbent on all. As a means of gaining a march on others, thrift is useful to the individual. But personal hoarding practised by a whole people could only lead to hardening the hearts of the poor and to their inflicting cruel wrong on those dependent upon them. Their small savings would, after all, be of little use to the respective owners. If they sought land, to what prices it would rise. If they placed their savings in the banks, they would only swell the resources of the capitalist by whom the banks are controlled. The field of employment would be limited by a reduced consumption of commodities, and the capitalist would secure a still larger proportion of the annual product of the nation. Clearly these are not the roads to national welfare, national progress, nor a healthy national life. They savour too much of that marvellous penny which, invested at compound interest of 5 per cent at the birth of our Lord, was to pay off the National Debt of Great Britain thirty times over in six hundred years, be beyond calculation in 1200, and beyond imagination in 1800.

The annual produce of every civilised nation is ample to supply the needs of all, and would leave a vast amount to spare. Many now receive their quota in gaols, asylums, workhouses, or through some degrading form of what is called charity. None, let us hope, are left to starve. Mr. Mulhall places the number of families in the United Kingdom in 1889 at 6,820,000, and tells us that they possessed an aggregate yearly income equivalent, if it were in coin, to twelve hundred and eighty-five million pounds sterling. The average to each family was £188; but the average is meaningless except for comparison with similar averages from year to year, or with the averages of other nations. If it could

The yearly production is enough to supply the needs of all, with a vast amount to spare.

be said that in no case did any family receive less than even £30 a year, with the rudest form of healthy shelter, there would still be the vast sum of ten hundred and eighty-five million pounds sterling to be fought for yearly and to keep alive the individual energy on which, as man is now constituted, the progress of the race and the nation must depend.

What will the coming century have to tell? Shall we ever have such a record from our statisticians? Who can tell? They have much to record now that would have seemed incredible a century ago. Who can say what will be impossible in the century to come? This much is certain. The statesman who can announce the assurance of this small sum to every family, will end the wail of the unemployed—the saddest wail of the day. Freedom of contract will then become a reasonable bargain between him who requires labour and him who will no longer have to sell at once or starve. There is enough for all and ample to spare. That is clear. The question is one of partition—in other words, of due taxation and due safeguards against abuse in every direction in which those safeguards can be taken. The difficulties of the problem are great, but the internal peace, the progress, perhaps even the independent existence of civilised nations are involved in its solution. Helpless misery, and the despair which helpless misery begets, are the deadliest foes with which nations can have to deal. When men believe that no change can be for the worse, when pessimism reigns supreme, the end is not far. That is the story of the past. Let us hope that the future, with its wonderful and increasing facilities for education, for discussion and for combination, will have a new and happier tale to tell.

CHAPTER III

NATIONAL WEALTH

THE national wealth is composed of the accumulated products of the labour—mental and manual—of the whole people. It includes every possession deriving utility from human labour and tending to supply the manifold needs of many-sided man. *(Definition of national wealth.)*

Individual wealth, on the other hand, consists of that particular portion of these products over which some person has acquired exclusive control. The control rests sometimes on the natural right appertaining to the direct producer, but is far *(Definition of individual wealth.)*

more frequently conferred by law from considerations of public policy. In all cases, the personal claim is subject to such regulation or limitation as the welfare of the nation may render desirable. The State has always a right to assume possession, a right implied in the protection which it gives, and without which property in any form could not exist. This right is only to be exercised in the National interests. In order to preserve unimpaired the confidence necessary to encourage industry, reasonable compensation is to be paid to those from whom the surrender is demanded.

<small>To be wealth, must embody human labour.</small> We believe that this definition will be found enough for all practical purposes. The chief point to be noted is the embodiment of human labour in all products that

can be included in the national wealth. Slaves, for example, were till recent times a valuable element of wealth to their owners. They were saleable at high prices and in large numbers. In the British Colonies, in the year 1834, they numbered 780,000, and their owners received from the British nation an average compensation of £26 for every slave then made free. In 1862 there remained in slavery in the Brazils more than $1\frac{1}{4}$ million of human beings, valued by the owners at £104,000,000 sterling. In 1864 nearly four millions of slaves were emancipated in the United States, representing a vast loss to their owners, and freed at the cost of a terrible expenditure in blood and treasure to the nation. In olden times slaves were of even greater price. Counted in our present money they ranged in Greece from £60 to £103 according to strength and skill. In Rome they ranged as labourers and mechanics from £50 to £150, while a first-class cook sold for £430, an actress for £820, and a physician for £1100. The population of the Roman Empire is variously estimated to have been from 100 to 120 millions. About half of these were slaves, and the sum which they represented to their owners must have been immense. Yet not one farthing of all these vast sums could be included in the national wealth. The slaves were not commodities and could not, like cattle, be consumed. As workers they created national wealth, but they would have done this to greater effect if free. Only the product of labour is national wealth. The labour power inherent in man, like the fertility inherent in the soil, the minerals buried in the mountains, the fish in the seas, the rivers naturally navigable, the climate giving health and strength, and all other natural advantages, are gifts of God to man. They are to be counted as resources, but only the products obtained from them can be counted as wealth to the nation. Vast portions of the most fertile parts of the earth are occupied to-day by communities ranking among the poorest because they fail to turn their great natural resources to account.

The only enduring and trustworthy sources of national wealth are soil, sea, and rivers possessed by the nation, together with the industries, arts, and manufactures to which their products give rise. Advantages of position, or security from risk of foreign

Soil, sea, and rivers the only trustworthy and enduring sources of national wealth.

invasion, may make a city or a country a central world mart, bring all nations trading at its door and great floating wealth to its people. But history teaches how precarious are such sources of wealth to a nation, how easily lost by deviation from established trade routes, by widespread improvements in methods of production or transport, and by the desire for self-dependence in other nations. Continued and increasing yearly production within a country is the only true source of national wealth. The only sound reliance of a nation and the only sure foundation of its strength must always be its own internal trade, the development of its own resources, and the consuming as well as producing power of its own prosperous people.

Personal savings can only form a

secondary element in the growth of national wealth. The primary element is the excess of production beyond the natural and ordinary demands for consumption—an excess of which the origin must be sought in the facilities given by science and invention. The national wealth takes innumerable forms. Food, clothing, ships, churches, schools, museums, and buildings of every kind and for every purpose, war material, and, in short, all that can serve for the maintenance of life and its enjoyment by the individual or for the safety and independence of the nation, are to be included in the nation's wealth. The greater part of these possessions is of a quickly perishable nature, and the whole call for constant care and renewal. A year or two of enforced idleness would see an end to available food

The sources of wealth and capital.

in the richest of nations. Very few years of similar cessation from work would send the most fertile fields back to wilderness, see cities perish and the most solid structures fall to ruin or decay. Man lives on the labour of the past. The labour of the present can only provide for the future, and must be supplied with the requisite support and materials until the commodities on which it is employed are made fit for the use of man. Hence the need of a reserve of food, clothing, implements, and the innumerable articles by which the labour employed in providing for the future may be supported and made as productive as possible. This reserve we call Capital, which is therefore a name for that portion of the national wealth used, or capable of being used, in the processes necessary for replacing waste and consumption, or for extending the national production.

The wealth of the United Kingdom was computed by Dr. Giffen as having been in the year 1885 equal in coin to the vast sum of £10,037,000,000 (ten thousand and thirty-seven millions) sterling. The yearly production in excess of consumption is estimated as equal to £200,000,000. If we add this so-called saving for four years, we may compute the national wealth in the year 1889 as equal to 10,800 million of pounds sterling. In that year the income was estimated from the tax returns equal in coin to 1285 millions, so that the accumulated wealth was about $8\frac{1}{2}$ times the yearly product and the yearly earnings of every kind which, together, are called income. Mr Mulhall, taking the tax returns for

Wealth of the United Kingdom.

1889, makes certain calculations which show that the earnings were—

From direct labour . .	£731,000,000
From Capital . .	554,000,000
	£1285,000,000

The earnings from Capital are given thus in detail.

FROM INTERNAL SOURCES

Land and Houses, . . .	£193,498,000
Mines and Quarries, Gas Works, Water Works, Canals, etc., .	24,801,000
Profits from Farming, from certain Professions and Business, and from Joint-Stock Companies	217,690,000
Profits from Railways . .	33,270,000
	£469,259,000

FROM EXTERNAL SOURCES

Investments in Public Funds	£21,096,000	
,,	Railways . 3,808,000	
,,	Other Securities 9,859,000	
,,	of various kinds 50,000,000	
		84,763,000
		£554,022,000

We have not at hand the figures showing the whole national wealth for that year (1889). Those for 1885, before referred to, will answer as well for explaining how that wealth was constituted. The amount it will be remembered was 1037 millions. The details were—

Houses and Buildings	£1,927,000,000
Farming and other Business and Industries	1,759,000,000
Land	1,691,000,000
Railways, British and Foreign	1,008,000,000
Foreign Loans and Investments	1,027,000,000
Furniture and Works of Art	960,000 000
Sundries	860,000,000
Public Property of various kinds	500,000,000
Mines, Quarries, Iron Works, Gas Works, Water Works, Canals, etc.,	305,000,000
	£10,037,000,000

The "sundries" probably include the gold and silver—the coin and coinable bullion—which in 1885 did not exceed 143 millions. The small proportion which the coin and coinable metals thus bore to the total wealth of the nation is a feature of the most noteworthy kind. That proportion was less than threepence halfpenny (3½d.) to every pound sterling of other property. We shall have occasion to call attention at greater length hereafter to this pregnant fact.

<small>National liabilities in United Kingdom and in Colonies contrasted.</small>

This vast wealth is of course subject to liabilities. There are the national and corporation debts and private debts of various descriptions to be met. When these liabilities are due to persons belonging to the country and residing in it, the total of the national wealth is not disturbed, though the partition of the annual product is materially affected. In Colonies, claims of this kind are generally held by persons who are non-resident. The wealth of the community is then proportionally diminished, and the payment of principal and interest can only be met by exportable products. In Colonies it becomes therefore of great importance to refrain from using borrowed capital except where it can be made to increase, adequately and directly, the sum of the annual production. If used for any other purposes, however desirable in themselves, the operation is full of hazard. The work done must be premature because it should have been deferred till the internal wealth of the community sufficed. This premature expenditure of borrowed capital is sure to lead to difficulty and confusion. If the expenditure be large the burden cannot fail to be seriously felt, and in many cases can only be borne by the participation—*nolens volens*—of residents and non-residents able to provide from other than colonial sources for the share in the burden which their colonial undertakings have to meet.

<small>Other evils of too rapid expenditure of borrowed capital.</small>

Other grave evils follow the too rapid introduction into a new country of borrowed capital that does not add sufficiently to its yearly product. The ordinary phrase "raising money by a Government Loan" is damagingly deceptive. The Government manufacture and export a certain number of interest-bearing and transferable debentures. Against this export the Custom House soon has to record an import of railway iron, of food, clothing, and innumerable commodities to be consumed or used while certain works are being executed or certain services being performed. Numbers of persons find employment for the time; prices become inflated (of land and houses especially); but if the expenditure is not directly reproductive its termination finds the colony with large liabilities to be paid for in exported produce, with numbers of people unemployed, with a falling trade and revenue, and with a reaction in prices that brings ruin upon all who had been forced to incur obligations based on the inflated scale. Population becomes unduly concentrated in the towns, especially where the borrowing has been for railways, and a wide disturbance of industrial, social, and political life is inevitable. These are lessons often taught but easily forgotten. They were deeply impressed on the United States in their younger days and have been as deeply impressed on many of the British Colonies by hard experience in recent times.

<small>Some investments of capital by the United Kingdom.</small>

Carefully compiled statements of the wealth and income of the United Kingdom make clear several points of great interest to the student of political economy. Among them is a statement showing how the sum of nearly 3500 millions of the national wealth was invested in the year 1882, and how the interest, amounting to £155,300,000, was produced. These investments may be classified as (1) in railways, and similar tangible wealth both at home and abroad; (2) in instruments of credit giving control over certain portions of yearly earnings or property within the United Kingdom; (3) in instruments of credit giving similar control over earnings or property abroad. The following is the list:—

	Millions.		Millions.
National Debts	769	Yielding	23·1
Railways	770	,,	33·2
Banks	270	,,	16·6
Mines and Iron Works	215	,,	11·8
Canals and Docks	94	,,	3·7
Gas and Water Works	72	,,	5·7
Telegraphs	30	,,	1·7
Insurance Companies	20	,,	1·2
Shipping	193	,,	9·7
	2433		106·7
Colonial Loans	148	,,	7·4
Indian Loans	154	,,	6·2
Indian and Colonial Railways	186	,,	9·3
Foreign Loans and Railways	570	,,	25·7
	3491		155·3

With clear conceptions of what is meant by national wealth, national capital, and national income, and of the essential difference between the solid, tangible substances of which they are composed and the instruments of credit by which these movements are controlled, many difficult questions will be more readily mastered.

<small>Misleading use of terms, and the great functions of credit in exchange.</small>

We must carefully avoid being misled by long used but inexact phrases. Among them none are more misleading than the terms "Cash" and "equivalent to Cash," applied without discrimination to coin and to certain instruments of credit. We must never lose sight of the very small proportion which coin and coinable bullion bear to the total of national wealth. In the year 1885 they did not exceed, as we have shown, $3\frac{1}{2}$d. in the pound. They did not represent 2s. 3d. in the pound of the year's income, and probably less than 6d. in the pound of the available capital. On the other hand, upon this comparatively small amount of specie enormous transactions depend. There are the 1500 millions invested in railways and joint-stock companies, the 769 millions in national and corporation debts, the 1000 millions of bank liabilities, the thousands of millions of stocks of all kinds and of all nations which are quoted in the lists of the London Stock Exchange, and the many hundreds of millions in shipping and factories, or otherwise employed in the agriculture and commerce of the United Kingdom. All these are supposed to depend for life and movement on less than 150 millions of what is called money—a sum which would be absurdly inadequate without the existing facilities for rapid exchange and the vast amount of credit by which the coin is supplemented. Credit does the great and real work of exchange. It is credit which makes so delicate and complex the fabric of national prosperity and even the national life. Without credit the mass of inert matter which forms the national wealth would remain inert, its power of movement and of exchange be lost, and the inducements to its renewal disappear.

<small>Vital importance of the small amount of specie.</small>

Small though the proportion of specie to the national wealth may be, it is the axle on which revolves the vast wheel that pours forth from bank reservoirs continual streams of credit to do the work of exchange. The commerce and the transactions of the whole United Kingdom are carried on by a proportion of credit to specie estimated variously at from 92 to 96 per cent. In London, with its great facilities for rapid exchange, the proportion is 98½ per cent, leaving only £1 : 10s. to be provided in coin for every hundred pounds of business done from day to day during the year. In the London Clearing-House, transactions amounting to 6500 million pounds sterling are settled during the year with less than 4 per cent in specie to liquidate the balances in each day's work. When Stock Exchange settlement days bring their quota, the clearing has reached seventy millions. To liquidate this last great sum less than three millions in specie are required.

So long as there is a belief that the requisite amount of specie will be forthcoming, credit is undisturbed and has full play. If that belief be in any way shaken, confidence begins to wane. If the waning *Panic if specie fall below a certain point.*

be not checked, a panic will follow. *Sauve qui peut* is then the cry. All are sellers eager to be the first to get rid of their dead commodities and obtain some part of the limited means of circulation in their place. Buyers are only to be found on the most ruinous terms. Down go prices. Obligations cannot be met. Failures follow. Factories close, industry of all kinds is stayed, masses of people are thrown out of employment, the painful savings of years disappear, exchange is paralysed and ruin widespread. Yet the wealth created by the nation's industry is all the time intact. It is stored in warehouses, factories, ships, and granaries, and exists in a thousand varied forms. It is there, but it is useless. Credit has ceased to give life and power of movement. The result is want in the midst of plenty and ruin in the face of vast material wealth. It is hard to believe this in accord with nature, or that a remedy cannot be found. Meanwhile we may safely conclude that no remedy will be forthcoming so long as a small quantity of the precious metals is the only foundation for commercial credit, and so long as that small quantity is still further limited in effect by placing it under the control of banks in whose coffers it is gathered, and who, in their turn, are controlled by the great monarchs of finance whose claims in time of trouble take precedence of all.

In these latter days a new factor is to be noted as exercising vast influence on finance. From nations, from public corporations, from joint-stock companies, and from many sources, have come million

Influence of national debts in creating private control of the credit circulation.

upon million of what are called liquid securities. The peculiarity of these securities is that, in addition to carrying a continuous interest they are commodities transferable at any moment for exchange with other commodities. The effect of these two qualities and of the confidence felt in their safety, is to place them in universal request as representatives of wealth, always productive in themselves and always "liquid," *i.e.* readily convertible into the commercial credit by which commodities are circulated. The market for these liquid securities is international in most cases, and in times of crisis they take practical command of what purchasing power may be left available. Governments jealously guard the royal prerogative of coining money and regulating the currency. Their operations are poor indeed in face of those of the holders of liquid securities who, to a very great extent, control the real circulating medium, and with it the industry, the commerce, and the wealth of nations.

CHAPTER IV

THE CREATION OF NATIONAL WEALTH

<small>Conditions for creating national wealth.</small>
SECURITY for life and property is the first essential to the appreciable creation of wealth. If personal, political, and intellectual freedom be added, with provision for the proper education of the people, we have conditions under which energy will be stimulated and progress carried to the full extent of which the resources of the country are capable.

<small>Transportation and fiscal protection.</small>
Facilities for internal and external communication extend the area of exchange, enlarge consumption, increase knowledge

and experience and all material incitements to production. In the same category may be included aid given by the State in protecting against external competition the industries and products congenial to the particular country with which the State is concerned. The old objection that such aid deludes capital into unprofitable channels and diverts it from profitable use, is based on an assumption that the capital of a nation—like the imaginary wages fund—is a fixed quantity in constant employment. With ordinary judgment in the selection of objects, the success of a national protective policy has been well proved in all countries. The industries of the United Kingdom were thus fostered in their days of weakness. In more recent times the beet sugar industry of Europe and the iron and steel industries of the United States of America are striking illustrations. Of course the policy is here regarded from a national and not from a cosmopolitan point of view. The federation of the world is still but a poet's vision.

<small>The East India Company as a chartered monopoly.</small>   Chartered monopolies have played their part in encouraging Adventurers to enter upon undertakings which called for large outlay with the prospect of only distant returns. Monopolies of this kind have always been disliked as containing germs of injury to the nation. They have been granted on fixed conditions and for a stipulated time, but neither conditions nor time limits have been sustained when powerful interests were concerned. The Chartered Association formed by amalgamating rival enterprises and long known as the United East India Company, was the greatest and

most remarkable of monopolies. Founded in the year 1600 by a few London merchants quarrelling with the Dutch East India Company over the supply of spices, its operations began in the islands of Malaysia. A bitter feeling arose between the Dutch and English, and finally in 1623 a massacre at Amboyna induced the English Company to transfer operations to India. A charter secured the legal monopoly of trade with the rich countries of the East, and for long years the Company guarded its monopoly by an armed navy which seized and confiscated the ships and property of what were officially called interlopers. The monopoly was retained for more than two hundred years. During all that time not a pound of tea, a yard of silk or cotton goods, not a pound of spice nor any other of the valuable commodities of the East, could be imported into any part of the British Empire except by or through this great trading and ship-owning company. In 1833 the trading privileges were withdrawn, but the government of the Indian Empire which the Company had built up by diplomacy and arms was left to its administration till the terrible mutiny of 1857 ended the Company and its rule together. Great Britain was forced to interpose. The mutiny of the Company's army was suppressed and the government of India assumed by the nation. The difference between its open rule in the spirit of a free people, and the rule of a close, money-making corporation, is to be seen in the prosperity of India and the increased life, activity, and social as well as material progress of the multi-typed Indian peoples.

New Zealand, in 1840, was saved by a smaller but somewhat similar company from becoming a French colony. The action of the Company forced the Imperial Government to take possession of those splendid islands just in time. The New Zealand Company differed so far from the East Indian that its object was to trade in land and not in goods. A chartered monopoly was not therefore required, but its primary object was the same—to make money for its shareholders. Against the good effected by the New Zealand Company must be placed its unscrupulous dealings for Maori land on the one side, and with British land buyers on the other. These dealings laid the sure foundation for the Maori wars and insurrections which retarded the progress of New Zealand, caused a large expenditure of

The New Zealand Company.

blood and treasure, and for many years dominated all other considerations in the politics of the colony. Chartered monopolies may do good, but history shows that they always require the closest watching, and that no corporation whose primary object is the making of money can be entrusted with the higher duty of governing a people. The economic gain is more than counterbalanced by the inevitable tendency to national demoralisation.

<small>Breaking up of tribal organisation and tribal rights to land.</small> Another necessary element in the growth of wealth is the breaking up of tribal organisation. Unfortunately this operation has always been coincident with the unconditional seizure of tribal lands by a powerful and organised few who steal a march on an ignorant and obedient people. Sooner or later this is followed by relieving the land

from the costs of public defence and its other public obligations, and transferring the burden to the industry of the nation. Acquiescence in this far-reaching conversion of original rights gave to them the sanction of time and custom. New interests have been created and thousands of "innocent third parties" involved. Radical changes become difficult, for they cannot fail to bring loss and perhaps great misery to many unoffending people. Hence the need of stifling any attempt at public wrong before it has time to bear fruit, and of resisting at the outset, however tempting it may be made to appear. Hence also the need of just consideration for the interests of others, and the wisdom of the moderation which this begets when we aim at redressing past wrongs or at readjusting economic relations.

Original land tenure in New Zealand.

In New Zealand the public lands were sold to the original purchasers without other conditions than those implied in every form of possession which owes its existence to the supreme authority of the State, and which would, without such authority, cease to be of value. Yet the exchangeable price of those lands, in both town and country, but in town especially, has been very greatly increased by the increase of population, by enlargement of the local markets, and by public works of all kinds executed at the cost of the whole people. Enormous gifts have thus been made to the owners of land at the expense of other sections of the community. The same tacit acquiescence has allowed time to sanction the original injustice of the policy, and has allowed the inevitable "innocent third party" to purchase the land with all its new privileges at a proportionate price. It should here be noted that the enhancement thus created in the price of land does not add an iota to the wealth of the community. It diverts to the owner the control over a larger share of the annual product of the general industry, but does no more.

The people who are rendered practically landless by loss of their tribal right of free occupation become entirely dependent on money in order to obtain even the simplest necessaries of life. One means of getting money is to sell the product of their home industry. When the growth of machine power and the rise in the price of land have driven home products out of the field, they are compelled to sell their labour power to others who own the machinery or the land,

<small>A landless people entirely dependent on money.</small>

and whose object is to purchase the labour power at a rate that will enable them to make as large a profit as possible for themselves. The buyer of the labour power has, almost universally, a glutted market in which to make his bargain. The seller must strike the bargain quickly or starve. This is the condition known, by an economic fiction, as freedom of contract, and upheld as one of the special rights of free men and the glory of a free nation.

<small>Beginning of wage dependence.</small>

Here we come to a point of the utmost importance. We see the beginning of the era of wage dependence, and that land on which a man can find shelter however rude —land from which he can obtain by his own labour the necessaries of life however simple —is the first necessity to free the wage dependents, as a class, from the absolute and entire need for money which makes their alleged freedom of contract a nullity and a farce. When land occupation is widely diffused thousands are freed from the necessity of earning money at every step, at every hour, and for every meal. The market is relieved from the cut-throat competition which reduces men to practical servitude, and which trades unions can only, within narrow limits and by endless struggling, partially counteract.

The old Guilds were widely different, and so were the circumstances of the time. Machinery had not then superseded personal skill, and the land was still comparatively open to all. The master and the apprentice—the employer and the employed—had common interests and were in constant personal intercourse.

The old English Guilds.

The opposition was between producer and consumer. There was little or none between producers themselves; nor was there a great mass of landless unemployed to be taken into account. The guilds met every need of the time. They ruled their respective crafts, and were always ready to unite with each other when the interests or privileges of any were threatened. Land concentration was a serious blow to guild organisation, threw large numbers on the labour market, and created a rift in the previously common interests of the employer and the skilled employed. Other conditions of life were changed, and the contest was no longer between producer and consumer, but between producers themselves. Production increased and the master and apprentice, losing their old relation, got out of touch with one another. Excellence in quality ceased to be the paramount aim in production, and a rivalry in cheapness took its place. The old Guilds died, and machinery has rendered impossible the restoration of anything like similar bodies except as rigid and obnoxious castes. Trade unions, which are unions of wage dependents purely, now stand opposite to similar unions of employers, while outside of them we find the most serious element of all, the helpless mass of unemployed. Scotch shipwrights used to say that one man too many will lower wages, but that half a dozen employers must be seeking men before the wages rise again. Acting on this belief they subscribed and sent to sea, or to other countries, the surplus man as soon as he appeared, but this was only a palliative and not a cure. More searching changes will be required to meet the altered conditions of modern life. These changes must strike at causes and not merely deal with effects, but from their nature and from the obstacles in their way they can only be gradually and carefully brought into operation.

<small>Objects to be kept in view.</small> To continue the increase of national wealth, but to free the process from all preventible misery to individuals, is the difficult problem. A full and complete knowledge of the conditions of production, of commerce, and of transportation will be indispensable to its solution. Well equipped commissions armed with full power of investigation would supply the best and readiest means. They would

supply the economist with sound data, but the statesman alone is able to judge how far proposed reforms are in accord with public opinion and suitable to the circumstances of the time. To thin the ranks of the unemployed and to render life tolerable to any who are left unemployed is at the heart of the question. Whether this be sought in wider land occupancy, in subsidies to societies acting as local agents for the State, or in both, or in some other measures yet to be suggested, the solution becomes more pressing daily.

Upwards of five centuries have passed since the Statute of Labourers interposed human law to distort the natural relations between labour and capital in England. The last four of these centuries have

Five centuries of struggle.

witnessed great extensions of colonisation and production, but among them the last half of the present century has outstripped all. Unhappily it cannot be denied that the same half-century has widened the original division between labour and capital and threatens to turn it into a yawning gulf. The universal application of machinery is the indisputable cause of the present position; yet without machinery, and without the aid of science man could not hope to meet the modern demands on production. Vast stores of the precious metals have been unearthed. They have given not only means for enlarged exchange, but are the richest of crops, gathered from small areas, always sure of a market, easily transported, and call for wonderfully little capital and a wonderfully great proportion of labour in their earlier production. They have thus been the means of effecting settlement and of concentrating population in lands which must otherwise have lain for centuries unused. Production has far outrun the needs of consumption, and the surplus accumulations are unprecedented in the history of mankind. From these accumulations comes the capital without which production could not be maintained, and without which national wealth would speedily shrivel.

Liberated by capital from the necessity of working for immediate returns, labour takes wider flight. Men, separated by thousands of miles from each other and ignorant even of each other's existence, work to a common end. The division

Power of labour aided by capital.

of labour consequent on the large scale of production causes each worker to attain the highest proficiency in his particular part. Materials brought from widely distant places are wrought into a complete fabric and fitted for the use of man. Neither labour alone, nor capital alone, could achieve these marvellous results. By their co-operation the great work of the world is done and progress made possible. Thus has the coracle of the ancient Briton grown through many stages to the ocean greyhound of to-day. The pack-bullock, itself an advance on the human carrier, is replaced even in African wilds by the railway. The powerful steam-thresher is substituted for the time-honoured flail, and the lagging sickle has given place to the reaping and binding machine with its lifelike movements and miraculous speed. In literature the costly papyrus of the learned Egyptian is represented by the myriad products of the printing press, and in Science the microscope, spectroscope, and photograph are disclosing secrets which Nature long withheld or only permitted man vaguely to guess. In war, the developments are still more striking. For the sling that slew Goliath we have the Maxim gun, while huge cannon and huge ironclads replace the battering rams and terrible triremes of all-conquering Rome.

These are a few of the marvels which human labour—mental as well as manual—has been able to achieve by the aid of capital. Without capital none of them would have been possible. The great lessons which

<small>National capital indispensable and its preservation the first consideration.</small>

they teach are that the capital of the nation must be preserved if the creation of wealth at its present level is to be maintained, and that it must be continually increased if the creation of wealth is to be extended, if the nation is to keep pace with others, and if its equality and independence are to be secured. Let what may betide, this is the central truth which must never be allowed to go out of mind. Will any reasonable man assert that capital cannot be so maintained and increased without reducing to practical servitude great masses of a people? Will any assert that the present partition of the nation's vast annual product is right or reasonable, that some few should have an embarrassing superabundance while millions are swept into poverty far worse, in its close packing and foulness, than the poverty of the poorest savages in God's creation?

To assert such a belief would be an insult to our understanding and to civilisation. Yet there are men who talk, argue, and act, as if remedy were impossible, and who are content to denounce as agitators and demagogues those who do not concur in their wretched and inhuman view. Such men, when in a position to wield power or to exert influence, are the real enemies of society. In their self-satisfaction they are blind to the peril before them. The masses are no longer incapable of combination. They are becoming rapidly educated, and the necessities of States are turning them into soldiers trained and disciplined. Science is placing new and terrible weapons at their disposal, *The worst enemies of progress and of society.*

and poverty, with its iron hand, may drive them to despair but cannot hold them in submission.

<small>The old political issues are played out.</small> The attention which the wisest of our statesmen now pay to what are called social questions is one of the encouraging features of the day. The old political issues are played out. They have cleared the field but can no longer take the lead in free nations. Thanks however to the work they accomplished, we have the greatest freedom in discussion leading to the formation of a healthy public opinion, with good ground for belief that the time is at hand when marked advance will be made.

That advance must be continued till the annual product of the nation is so partitioned that the needs of a healthy life, however rude and simple, shall be assured to every one from whom the nation claims allegiance — which, at need, means life. Then may we hope to see the gulf between labour and capital disappear. Then, with immunity from degrading poverty and with the disappearance of a permanent pauper mass, we should cease to hear proposals for violent social change based upon an ideal of human nature lofty but, in the present stage of evolution, imaginary and unreal. With this great end gained, further timely reforms could well be left to the intelligence and the good feeling of a patriotic and prospering people.

CHAPTER V

CAPITAL AND CREDIT

Definition of Capital.

CAPITAL is that portion of a nation's wealth devoted, or capable of being devoted, to the renewal and increase of production. Capital may be dormant or active. The diamond for instance is dormant when used as a jewel, but made active directly in a rock-drill or indirectly by exchange with foreign countries for material or machinery to be used for productive purposes. Capital, being part of the national wealth, can only consist of the products of human labour. Gold and silver form but a small proportion of these products, but their importance is enhanced by their use for coin, for expressing price, and for regulating the amount of commercial credit available as a substitute for coin in the transfer of commodities.

In some form, Capital must have existed from the time when men began to feel the need of making provision for to-morrow. Individuals may acquire Capital by abstinence from consumption, but if the saving be from the product of a man's own labour the amount cannot be large. To the powers of production conferred by inventions in machinery and by the applications of Science, we owe the great accumulations of Capital in modern nations. They who own this Capital are comparatively few, but fewer still are they by

Origin of Capital.

whom it is controlled. The ownership or control would be of comparatively little moment if it were not for the dominating influence of Capital in regulating the partition of the annual product of the nation. Therein lies the trouble, a trouble growing yearly, and already so great as to be almost incapable of exaggeration.

Power of machinery in production.

To illustrate the enormous power of machinery and of improved methods of production, transport, and distribution, let us take some of the computations made by the well-known American Statistician, Mr. Edward Atkinson. He computes that 1000 people are supplied with bread for a whole year by human labour equivalent only to that of seven men working for three hundred days. This estimate, be it understood, includes all the processes of cultivating, reaping, threshing, and carrying the wheat to the mill, of converting it into flour, carrying the flour 2000 miles to market, and there making it into bread ready for the consumer. In the iron industry he computes the labour of one man working for three hundred days as equivalent to the labour employed in turning out 50 tons of iron ready for use, including the mining for the coal required for smelting and all operations from the extraction to the final preparation of the ore. The average yearly consumption of iron in the United States is reckoned at 5 cwt. per head, so that the three hundred days' labour of this one man would supply 200 people. In like manner, the labour equivalent to that of one man for three hundred days supplies cotton cloth for 250 persons or woollen cloth for 300, while in a boot and shoe factory it meets the requirements of 1000 persons for a year.

<small>Machines displacing human skill.</small>
In these operations each person is confined to a part, and often an insignificant part, of the whole work. Each becomes a mere attendant on the machine which guides the tool and replaces human skill in that direction. Beyond his own particular task, each worker is as ignorant as a person who never entered the factory. Among the thousands in boot factories there are probably none who could make a boot or shoe complete. Machinery is rapidly displacing human skill and human labour in every calling. Even the printer is vigorously attacked, and in face of composing machines and distributing machines must sooner or later, in the present form, cease to exist.

In the business of transportation, railways and great steamships are superseding all other methods. Enormous cargoes are carried over many thousand miles with regularity and speed. Comparatively few trained seamen are required, and similar changes on a great scale are effected by machinery in every branch of human industry. They tend to make labour more dependent upon Capital. They tend to drive out of the field all but the great capitalists, and to divide among the few that are left a continuously increasing share of the annual production. They tend to drive back into the ranks of labour a yearly increasing number to swell the competition for employment and lessen the individual share of the product. They tend to the use of less labour in production,

Labour becoming more dependent on capital.

and thus to leave so much more of the product to the controller of the Capital.

<small>Small proportion of labour in cost of production.</small>

These results are constant and continuous in production on the great scale in our modern industries. Coal-mining, for example, is an industry more than commonly dependent on human labour. Yet it has been computed that a rise in wages of 10 per cent adds only 2d. to 4d. per ton to the cost of the coal. This would make existing wages range from 1s. 8d. to 3s. 4d. for every ton of coal, and probably 2s. 6d. would be a fair average. In iron-mining the cost of labour is relatively as small. Yet other dues of different kinds paid to the land owner, for permission to mine or to get access to the land, are estimated by Sir Isaac Lowthian Bell at 3s. 6d. per ton in the Cleveland district, at 6s. in Scotland, and at

6s. 3d. in Cumberland, while in Germany they are only 6d., in France 8d., and in Belgium 1s. 4d. Mr. R. M'Ghee of Glasgow tells of a blast furnace which turned out 600 tons of iron per week. The dues of various kinds paid to owners of the mining and adjacent lands absorbed £202 per week, while the labour, including the manager, cost only £95. An inquiry into the relative proportions which labour and other outlays bear to the total cost in various branches of modern production would be of great value, but could only be satisfactorily undertaken by bodies endowed with the powers of a Royal Commission.

The total subversion of old conditions effected by modern machinery is clear. It is equally clear that without the aid of machinery, the gigantic demands of modern

Machinery power of the United Kingdom.

civilisation could not be met, and the commerce and wealth of the world would speedily shrink to their old dimensions. The question is whether the undoubted benefits from the use of machinery cannot be more widely and more reasonably distributed. The grandeur of the subject will be felt by all who are aware of the enormous part played by machinery in the work of the modern world. In the United Kingdom the machine power, inclusive of that employed in transport, is estimated by Mr. Mulhall as equivalent to the working capacity of 160 millions of adult men, while the whole of the actual living human producers of both sexes and all ages do not exceed twelve millions. Thus, for every million human workers of all ages and kinds there are thirteen millions of full-grown iron slaves, whose needs for subsistence are small, whose powers of production are gigantic, whose consumption of commodities is almost inappreciable, and who are not called upon to provide for themselves in old age or in time of need by devoting part of the product of their labour to societies for that purpose. The slave power of the old Roman Empire and its crushing contest with free labour seem small indeed when contrasted with the overwhelming power of these iron slaves and their effect on modern industrial life.

The great accumulations of personal wealth, and the clearly marked line between its owners on the one hand and the poverty-stricken masses on the other, assumed its present definite form during the French wars of this century, when Great Britain with a population of seventeen or eighteen

Crystallisation into present extremes of rich and poor.

millions, all told, found herself almost sole owner of the machinery power of the world. Machinery was a comparatively small power in those days, but added practically to her population some sixty or seventy millions of men, and enabled her, with the monopoly of markets secured by her naval supremacy, to face a world in arms and to perform feats of which we are still proud. From that time the commercial has replaced what remained of the old feudal spirit and has regulated the relations of man with man. From that time we may date the crystallisation of rich and poor into the "two nations" of Disraeli's *Sybil*, and the dangerous extremes of superabundant wealth and squalid poverty which the nation still exhibits. Capital then began to assert its all-controlling power in the partition of the year's product, and Capital, though it may be owned by thousands in greater or less amount, is controlled by the few who take for themselves the giant's share, and leave to the rest the crumbs that fall from their table. The real control is not with the actual owners of Capital, but with the lords of credit who are masters of the money market and of the industrial world. Let us consider what Credit means, what work it does, and how that work is done.

Credit may be divided into three classes, commercial, landed, and financial. Commercial Credit is exclusively a bank creation, and the only credit possessing a direct purchasing power available in effecting exchanges of commodities of every kind. It takes form in drafts, promissory notes, *Commercial credit paper, its character, functions, and power.*

cheques, and other readily transferable documents circulated by banks to the extent of five or six times the whole coin in the country. They need only retain in their coffers coin or coinable bullion enough to meet all likely demands for the settlement of balances of account at home or for the payment of debts abroad. In theory, commercial credit is always represented by exchangeable commodities awaiting consumption or in course of renewal and completion for use in the more distant future. In either contingency, when the commodities are exchanged, or in ordinary language when they are sold, the old credit is cancelled and a new credit created in its place. Thus the ball is set rolling. It continues to roll so long as confidence is felt that, behind the credit, there is sufficient coin to meet all likely demands for settlement of the balances to which we have referred. When Commercial Credit is turned largely from its rightful purposes or trenched upon by other than dealers in commodities which are to be replaced when consumed, derangement is sure to follow. The power of the banks to issue credit is then decreased, what is called "bank accommodation" is restricted, and a restriction of business in every branch, more or less serious in extent, must result. The distinguishing feature of Commercial Credit is its direct purchasing power. It is the only credit medium available in exchange transactions of every kind.

Landed credit is peculiar and exceptional. Its sphere of action is limited, because landed credit has no direct purchasing

Landed credit.

power in exchange. Land can be used to take toll from all who are compelled to seek its acquisition, or who seek it for pleasure or other purposes. It can be made to bring a yearly revenue to its owner, but in itself land is not a commodity, cannot be consumed and then replaced by human labour, and cannot be distributed among buyers widely distant from one another as with ordinary commodities. He therefore who buys land or who lends upon its security parts with so much direct purchasing power, and may derive from the investment an annual income but cannot rely upon being able to reconvert it into commercial credit at need. This peculiarity is well understood at the great reservoirs and manufactories of credit, the banks. They welcome the landed proprietor as a customer, but take care that he shall only have the use of their credit to a very limited amount. Therein lies the great distinction between landed and commercial credit. We have throughout used the term commercial credit. Market credit or Bank credit would answer as well, but in any case nothing could or does mislead more than the terms "Cash," "Convertible into Cash," and "Equivalent to Cash" so constantly employed. They are only figurative, and come to us by tradition from a time when cash and coin were synonymous. We use them still, just as we speak of the sun rising and setting although the real movements of the planetary world have long been well and commonly known.

The third, the most powerful and the all-controlling form of Credit, is the financial.

Financial credit, the most powerful of all. This rests chiefly on mortgages of the national yearly product, and is secured on the whole wealth of the nation. The greater that wealth and the national power to maintain it against all possible enemies, the stronger the credit of the mortgages which are given in the various forms of what is called National Debt. Similar mortgages are issued by joint-stock companies, and by municipal or other public corporations. Many of these are accepted readily within the nation to which they are well known, but a distinctive feature of sound national obligations is their ready saleability in all the markets of the civilised world. They are not only sought on account of the interest they bear, which makes them revenue producers more certain than even the land, but for use as commodities transferable at any time and convertible into commercial credit like other commodities. Hence these securities are called liquid, and are eagerly sought by the great monarchs of finance, to whom they are so useful that they bring prices which put them out of the reach of the smaller investor dependent on the interest for his yearly income. Liquid securities thus bring an income while their holder sleeps, and can be converted into purchasing credit when other commodities are for the time unsaleable. For these reasons liquid securities are all powerful as controllers of the credit and of the industry and commerce of a nation. Here we may also note the grave change in a nation's currency when paper money, issued in times of stress, is afterwards funded. The free circulation of the country is by so much diminished, and a power over what is left falls into the hands of the holder of the liquid securities into which the Government notes that had performed the function of commercial credit are now converted. In transactions of this nature the Government receive nominally a certain amount in cash in return for the mortgages which they give on the wealth of the nation. In reality the Government receive only a certain amount of commercial credit issued by the banks and passed back to them in due course. A small proportion of gold may also pass for transmission abroad, but this is exceptional, and against it must be placed the proportion of gold paid perhaps by foreign purchasers of the new bonds.

In relation to this point it will be

interesting to glance at the operations of the United States Treasury with regard to the twenty million pounds sterling required by the law of 1882 to be kept in gold for redemption of notes which are issued as legal tender and received in payment of customs duties. The gold is practically part of the currency being represented by notes in circulation, and is only used to redeem these notes when they are presented. After redemption new notes are issued in accordance with the same law, as soon as possible. The object of the compulsory reissue is apparently to avoid a contraction of the currency. The gold which has been paid out by the Treasury to redeem the notes is not necessarily put into circulation. It may be sent abroad, or hoarded within the

The recent operations of a syndicate with the Treasury of the United States.

country to take advantage of the tempting opportunity which the arrangement offers to speculators on a large scale. The notes are issued in the ordinary course of Treasury disbursement, but the gold to meet them when presented at the Treasury for payment is not always forthcoming. The Treasury has to publish the state of its reserves, and when the statement shows a deficiency of gold the holders of the notes see that they are practically inconvertible. A want of confidence and a derangement of commerce would be the result if a remedy were not quickly found. A crisis of this kind which occurred in February 1895 is worth special notice.

<small>Agreement made with the syndicate.</small> Let us bear in mind that the United States has a population approaching seventy millions and is recognised as the wealthiest

of the world's nations. According to Mr. Mulhall its accumulated wealth is equivalent to a sum in coin of 13,000 million pounds sterling. Its available machinery is equivalent to the labour power of upwards of 225,000,000 of adult men. In education alone it spends yearly thirty-five million pounds sterling, while it pays in pensions to those who served in the Civil War an even larger sum. This great, rich, and populous nation found that the Treasury reserve in gold above referred to had fallen at the beginning of 1895 ten millions sterling below the required amount. How to get that comparatively small sum was a great difficulty. Finally the Government fell into such dire straits as to be reduced to the necessity of throwing itself into the hands of a syndicate of capitalists, American and British. This small syndicate controlled £120,000,000 sterling, and its power could not therefore be doubted. The instruments which enabled it to control this vast Capital must have been in the nature of liquid securities or of existing commercial credits belonging to themselves, or placed by others through the banks under their control. The syndicate supplied the Government with the requisite ten millions in gold in return for national bonds at a price which enabled them to resell at a profit estimated at two and a half to three million pounds sterling.

The Treasury, thus relieved, was reduced to the humiliating position of further asking from the syndicate, as part of its bargain, a guarantee that the gold in the Treasury, for which the nation had paid so dearly, should not be allowed to fall below the required twenty millions for six months following the transaction. In other words, the syndicate would themselves refrain from operating and would prevent other speculators from operating upon the notes, from using them for payment of duties instead of using gold, and from hoarding the gold or otherwise reducing the Treasury to the same straits within the few weeks or months that might be necessary to complete such operations. Here is a text from which many an economical sermon might be preached, but we are content to leave it for reflection by the intelligent reader. Not the least significant feature is the enormous amount of Capital which this small

Treasury compelled to put itself under the syndicate's wing.

syndicate claimed, and was admitted, to control.

<small>The State must recover control of the currency in all its forms.</small>　One of the great economical problems of the day is the recovery by the State of the real control of the national currency in all its forms, and as far as possible the free issue of that currency direct to the holders of the consumable commodities which it is designed to be the means of circulating. The conditions of the problem are complex, and it is trammelled by the number of "innocent third parties" who have been entangled in the meshes created by past wrongdoing and past error. The closest investigation and most careful deliberation will be called for in meeting this need. One thing cannot be made too clear or be too often repeated. However or by whomsoever the nation's Capital may

be controlled, whether it be left to individuals or, as some desire, to the State, the watchful preservation of that Capital and due provision for its yearly increase are indispensable for the progress of the nation and the maintenance of its independence and civilisation. It is difficult to see how the State, or how State officials, could be entrusted with duties so difficult and delicate and requiring an almost superhuman disinterestedness. Nor can so perilous an experiment be necessary. Other means nearer at hand must first be tried to prevent the abuses of Capital which too often blind us to the all-important functions which it must perform. Taxation on sound and equitable principles offers one means, and the readiest, of effecting reform. The diminution of liquid securities and depriving them as far as possible of the peculiar double character which makes them liquid, offers another.

<small>Inequality of sacrifice in present taxation.</small>

At present, taxation takes a certain percentage from the necessities of one and the same percentage from the superfluities of another. The old economists called this equality. The new economists give it a very different name. Labour, whose return in money must be always small, should be relieved from taxation both on its necessaries and few poor comforts or luxuries to the utmost extent possible. Accumulated wealth should gladly take a larger share of the burden. Due provision should be made for the maintenance, in times of involuntary idleness, of that reserve of the industrial army which we too often hear of as the unemployed. How far machinery should be made, and could be made, to contribute to this elementary need in good government can only be settled by full inquiry, but that labour should share more largely with Capital the greatly increased national product is manifestly fair, reasonable, and necessary. The State has limits which confine its operations, but within those limits it must not fear to act where the public welfare calls for action. Any industry or undertaking capable of management by systematic regulations and with the most unreserved publicity, may be regarded as within its ken. More especially does this apply to industries in which competition may have reduced the workers to misery in order that their employer, whether a sweater, a dock, railway, or tramway company, for example, may live or thrive.

A nation must be its own master.

The programme thus briefly outlined is no light one. An educated public opinion and an educated people could alone render it practicable. Forcing or attempts at forcing can only end in failure and in the reaction which is the worst effect that failure can produce. One condition is clear. The nation that would aim at such reforms must make itself its own master. The wages of its people, their hours of labour, and their whole welfare, must be regulated by their own sense of what is fitting and right, and not by the habits and ideas of competing nations. To this end the home trade of a prosperous and largely consuming people must be the first consideration, and the foreign trade must take a secondary place.

Finally let us hope that the day is at hand when a new motive power will restore much of the old domestic production which steam destroyed. Electricity promises to be that power, and to be capable of being made the great equaliser in production, reconstructing industrial methods and quietly rearranging industrial society. Is electricity, like steam, to fall under individual control, or is it to be held by the nation for the equal benefit of all its people? Already the Falls of Niagara are being captured and new vested interests being created. Very soon "the innocent third party" will block the way with claims for compensation, and with obstruction so great as to be long insuperable. Electricity, with its unimaginable possibilities, ought not to be allowed to gorge the few and become a means of further degradation to the mass. Every single member of the nation, however small his

The new motive power.—Shall it be the servant or master of the people?

wants may be, should command this new aid to industry as freely and as cheaply as the richest of his fellow-countrymen. The difference between administration in that spirit by the State, and administration in the spirit of personal gain by joint-stock companies, needs no demonstration. We are on the eve of a new era of prodigiously increased production. New possibilities are opening, and we have before us the simple issue whether this new power shall be the oppressive master or most valued servant of the people. Every man wishing well to his kind and with faith in human progress can have but one hope and give but one reply.

CHAPTER VI

JOINT-STOCK COMPANIES

AMONG the artificial elements introduced into our civilisation, none probably are more pregnant with danger than the joint-stock companies, which threaten to eliminate personal independence and human sympathy from much of the national life. Among these companies we must give a foremost place to the banks, who hold the purse-strings and control the commercial currency of the nation. Their power is felt in all the affairs of daily life, and that

Power of joint-stock companies.

power is wielded by the few who control bank operations.

<small>Principles and practice of joint-stock companies.</small>
Joint-stock companies, from beginning to end, are the creations of human law. Nature has nothing to do with them, and they have nothing to do with Nature. They are simply money-making machines, free from the feelings and sympathies which, in these days of unrestricted competition, are a recognised weakness in business life and impediments to personal success. The management of these companies is secret, and their leading principle to crush out rivalry and secure the greatest possible monopoly in any business which they have to undertake. Live and let live is no part of their policy, and would be regarded as a principle altogether childish if it were foolishly proposed to

them. Men and women outside of the company are so much material from which money may be made and they are no more. Their own shareholders practically delegate unchecked power to the directors by the manner of voting and by the certainty that if any of them ventured to find fault the rest of the shareholders would resent his action as depreciating the price of their shares in the market. These are the principles and this is the practice of the joint-stock companies which, from their number and power, give the tone to the commercial world, and force all to act likewise or face the risk of bankruptcy.

Joint-stock company formation received its strongest impulse from the well-intentioned Act which limited the liability of shareholders, but which experience has

<small>Present position of joint-stock companies.</small>

shown only serves to guard the wealthy speculator from too injurious loss while luring the man of smaller means to ruin. In 1885 the number of these companies in the United Kingdom was 13,328, and their registered Capital 775 millions sterling. In 1895 they numbered 18,361, with a paid-up Capital of 1035 millions. The cry is still they come. In New Zealand, with its small population of 700,000, no fewer than 103 companies were registered during a single year. Their business was of all kinds, including newspapers, fishing, dairying, butchering, boot-making, mining, general trading, and confectionery-making, but their single object was to make money by hook or by crook for their promoters in the first instance and then, if possible, for their shareholders. These companies have become a power in all civilised countries, making money for a few, but bringing thousands directly and indirectly to dependency or ruin. Undoubtedly the principle of co-operation on which they are based has done good in many cases, and is capable of more. The bane is in their legal incorporation, the secrecy of their management, the powers they are allowed to wield, and their freedom from the full consequences of their own actions which all men have to face. A little of the company formation may have done good. Too much of it is rank poison.

The great gains of the greatest of joint-stock companies, the "Honorable, the United Company of Merchant Adventurers trading to the East Indies," stimulated the formation of others in every direction.

<small>Companies denounced in 1655.</small>

The growing tendency was roundly denounced by Sir John Culpepper in the Parliament of 1655. They were "nests of wasps," "swarms of vermin overspreading the land." They were likened to the frog plague of Egypt. They "swarmed in our houses," and "we cannot buy even our clothes without their brokerage." The commonwealth was "almost hectical with these pests," and there was much more in a similarly vigorous strain. Had Sir John Culpepper lived in these more enlightened days he would probably have seen it wiser to be a director than a denouncer, and might have been a valued member of one of the numerous boards for which M.P.'s—especially titled—are in good demand. Times have changed and men change with them. To use an excellent business maxim, if we wish to make money we must go where money is and do as money does. If not, we must go to the wall and face the merciful bankruptcy laws which money-makers and companies have provided.

Companies of the joint-stock kind (limited) overshadow all lands, and their tremendous power must be curtailed in some way if money is not entirely to displace manhood in regulating the affairs and deciding the destiny of nations. Perhaps, as some of the Socialists say, they are but preparing the way by pooling and concentration, for the State to take the place of all that can be managed with perfect publicity. Doubtless many can be so managed as are the Post Office, Railways, Telegraphs, Schools, Water Works, Gas

Power of companies a public danger.

Works, Trust Agencies, Life Insurance, and numerous other services which were long considered as only suitable to be exploited for private gain. But any measures in this direction can only stand a chance of success when in accordance with existing social conditions and a well-matured and ripened public opinion. Society cannot be recast at a blow without incalculable mischief and the certainty of reaction as the only chance of repairing the mischief when done.

Company and bank capital and its constitution.

It is hardly necessary to say that the term Cash, usually applied to the "paid up" Capital of these joint-stock companies, is misleading. Capital consists of tangible commodities, and few of the great companies are burdened with these, especially at their formation. They acquire the control of a certain amount of commercial credit derived from the banks, who are its creators, depositaries, and dispensers. With that credit they can control the movement of commodities in their own country and in countries far away. With that credit they can bring food, clothing, and materials from the most distant quarters to the spot where they are needed at the time. The banks, who are themselves the most powerful of all joint-stock companies, issue Commercial Credit to an average amount of seven hundred million pounds sterling in the United Kingdom. They hold against it specie equivalent at the outside to one shilling in the pound. So long as the paper thus issued comes and goes and keeps in circulation, all is well. If the circulation be impeded, let the cause be what it may, a shrinkage in the operations of the banks must follow. If from any adverse circumstances the shrinkage continue too long or go too far, the bank is left to face its liabilities with a small amount of coin and with large credit assets not capable of exchange, because the medium for effecting that exchange has, for the moment, disappeared. Consequently, as the bank cannot at once pay all, it is forced to suspend altogether. The doors are closed, and the assets must wait the revival of commercial credit and the renewed circulation of credit paper, to be again negotiable and turned to account. Inevitable delay and loss to a greater or less extent is the result. Thus we see how vital to the existence of a bank is the credit which enables its paper to be kept in circulation and causes its coffers to be continually replenished by the deposit of other people's money or credit, for the bank to rise.

The Bank of England is the greatest and most venerable of banks so far as age and standing go. Others in other countries preceded it, but their spheres of action were limited and their power was small. The Bank of England on the contrary is not only the centre of finance for the United Kingdom but for the whole British Empire, while indirectly its influence is felt throughout the world. Its position is exceptional in so far that it holds the cash of numerous other banks, who keep with it what is called a drawing account, instead of keeping the cash in their own coffers. They operate upon this drawing account for the settlement of balances in the daily bank clearances and in other matters. A glance at the history and

The Bank of England.

position of the Bank of England will be useful.

<small>Origin of the Bank of England.</small>
In 1694 war expenditure had grown to big figures through the massing into nations of the several European States and the permanent substitution of paid standing armies for the older feudal gatherings of fighting men. Money was required, and a new mode of raising it by "funding" was devised. Mortgages were given on the existing wealth and the future industry of the nation. These were represented by documents which bore interest just as land bore rent, but they possessed an additional characteristic of great value. They were converted into commodities by being made transferable like other commodities. They were capable of transfer at any time, and were removable to any place or country.

The original parties to their purchase were soon lost to view, and the "innocent third party," who had purchased and paid well for the privileges attached to the documents, took their place. The original equity of the transaction was thus put out of court, for that was a point with which the new holder had no concern. These were the circumstances under which certain merchants of London agreed with the Government to lend £1,200,000, on condition that they should receive a charter giving them the exclusive right to open a bank of issue to be called the Bank of England; that they should receive 8 per cent interest yearly on the loan; that the Bank should do all the financial business of the Government, and should receive for that work £4000 per annum. Thus the National Debt of the

United Kingdom and the Bank of England started together.

<small>Opening of the Bank of England and of first joint-stock banks.</small>

The assured income of the Bank at starting was £100,000 a year, and it possessed a monopoly of the issue of notes payable on demand. The doors were opened on 27th July 1694 and business was begun. The charter was for a limited period, but has since been extended, from time to time, under varying conditions and with new loans to the Government. When the debt had increased to fourteen and a half millions, the Bank was authorised to issue notes to that amount against it, but the interest was reduced to $2\frac{3}{4}$ per cent on the loan. The monopoly lasted till 1826. Till that year no partnership for banking business of any kind could be formed by more than six persons, and no notes payable on demand could be issued in any case. In 1826 the law was amended. Partnerships of more than six persons could be formed, but they were not to issue notes payable on demand within sixty-five miles of London—a condition which retained practically the monopoly of the Bank of England in this respect for all England and Wales. In 1834 the first joint-stock bank, the London and Westminster, was opened. Since then their multiplication has been so great that they now number 155, including twenty-eight colonial banks with offices in London, and they have nearly 5500 branches in the United Kingdom, the Colonies, and other parts of the Empire.

The Bank of England has always taken

Present position of the Bank of England.

and still takes the lead. It has usually about twenty-five million pounds worth of bank notes in circulation, of which fourteen and a half millions represent the national indebtedness. The remainder is issued against gold coin or bullion in the Bank's cellars. Besides the liability for notes, the Bank holds forty-six to fifty millions of deposits, which include the deposits of other banks previously referred to. The liabilities are thus about seventy-three millions, against which there is generally thirty-six to thirty-seven millions held in coin and bullion. It pays dividends ranging from 8 to 9 per cent, and its stock is eagerly bought in the open market at £330 for every £100. Such, in 1895, is the great Bank established on a capital comparatively small two hundred years ago.

The other joint-stock banks began their career one hundred and forty years after the Bank of England. They have shown marvellous powers of expansion during the sixty years of their existence. We have already given their number and the number of their branches. They hold deposits and owe on various accounts about seven hundred and fifty millions sterling. If we include their liability to shareholders, the total would be nearly one thousand millions. To meet this they have a vast mass of credit paper representing, or supposed to represent, consumable commodities, and they have also cash "in hand and at call" stated at one hundred and eighty-five millions. How much of the cash "at call" is mixed up in the accounts of bank with bank or with private debtors

Present position of joint-stock banks.

is not clear, but we may safely assume that the actual cash does not exceed 3s. in the pound of their liabilities. Their shares vary much in market price, but in some cases the dividends paid are large and the prices of shares high—the dividend being 20 per cent and the paid-up shares of £10 selling at nearly £40.

<small>Foreign and private banks in the United Kingdom.</small>   We have not included in the above figures the seventeen foreign banks operating in London with liabilities stated at one hundred and ten millions, nor the forty private banks still in existence with liabilities of seventy-one millions. Enough, we hope, has been said to give a clear conception of the position, character, and work of these powerful companies who control the coin and credit without which commerce would speedily come to an end,

the world return to barter, and the inducements to production sink to a minimum.

To complete the picture let us now cast a glance at the National Debt of the United Kingdom, the fountain from which issues a stream of the liquid securities that play a powerful part in the credit world. In 1694 the Debt began at £1,200,000. In 1702 it had grown to £12,750,000. In 1756 it was £75,000,000, and at the beginning of the French wars in 1792 had swelled (chiefly through the struggle with the revolted American Colonies) to £240,000,000. In 1815 — only twenty years later — it reached the highest point, 861 millions, and has since been reduced to less than 700. In 1850 the national debts of the whole civilised world were less than 1800 millions. In 1882 they had risen to 5200 millions, and are much larger now, but the exact figures we have not at hand.

<small>Rates at which the national bonds were sold.</small>

With regard to these debts, it must be remembered that they are almost invariably incurred in times of national difficulty and at great loss. The worse the straits of the nation, the harder becomes the grip of the great dealers in credit whom we call financiers, and the less does patriotism stand in their way. Business is business, and the business of the financier is to add all that he can to his store. The nation is not his affair and must take care of itself. The debt of Great Britain was incurred to a very great extent by giving mortgages over the national wealth and future industry, at the rate of £160 at 3 per cent interest for every £100 which the financier paid. Nor was even the £100 paid in coin

Nominally it was in cash. In reality it was in commercial credit paper emanating from the banks, passed by them to the financier, and rapidly returned to the original creator. The interest on national debts is unfortunately but a part of the consequences of the issue in their present form. That is a measurable burden which might be fairly adjusted and borne with comparative ease. But their added character as exchangeable commodities, having from their nature the most commanding position among all commodities, gives them a powerful control over the currency, and with it over the industry, the commerce, and even the policy of a nation.

They who control these and similar securities are the modern monarchs of finance. The Crœsus of the nineteenth

<small>The modern monarchs of finance.</small>

century wallows not in gold. He floats in clouds of paper as powerful in their attraction of commodities as the magnet in its attraction of the metals subject to its sway. Small need has he to trouble himself with care of gold or silver, or with the burden of other commodities. Liquid securities bring them at his call, and meanwhile bring him a profit while he sleeps. This is a weighty characteristic of national debts, and a light in which their incidence is well worth study and regard. This is the characteristic which enables them to give control over the banks, and through them over the great joint-stock company world. If the growth of these companies be not checked, their powers materially curtailed, and the persons connected with them made to bear the fullest responsibility, they must become a menace to liberty and to the nations whose industrial operations they threaten to monopolise and, in the most sordid spirit, to control.

CHAPTER VII

VALUE AND PRICE

<small>Value, price, and the precious metals as commodities and measures of value.</small>

INDISCRIMINATE use of the terms value and price is a fruitful source of confusion. Value, or worth in use, may exist without price. But price, or worth in exchange, cannot exist without value. Fresh air and fresh water, the light and heat from the sun, the right to fish in seas and rivers, the delights of beautiful scenery, the surface and subterranean products of the earth, are of inestimable value to man. None of them can have price till assigned for exclusive use in such form as to make assignment transferable. Then they become commodities, perhaps intangible as the right to fish, perhaps tangible as the fish when caught. In either case a commodity is the result of human action in some form, and is therefore said to acquire its character from embodying human labour. In primitive societies commodities are exchanged directly for each other, and there is no common measure to indicate the ratios in which they thus exchange. In more advanced communities a common measure is created; the measure now in use being either gold stamped as coin, or gold and silver so stamped, or silver alone. These metals have therefore a double character. They are commodities deliverable as commodities, with the additional function of measuring and expressing as coin the respective ratios of commodities to each other in exchange, which ratios we call their price.

The value of all commodities consists in their utility either to mankind at large, or to a particular nation, or to a particular individual, in ministering to their respective needs or desires. The political economist is concerned chiefly with their price, as that is the point on which questions of exchange and of production turn.

Illustrations of value and of price. Let us take, as illustrations, the egg of the great Auk of which the sale was reported in the *Times Weekly* of 5th July 1895, the great collection of postage-stamps sold at about the same time, and the then current price of wheat. The egg was sold to the International Fur Store for £173 : 5s. The postage-stamps were sold to M. Ferdinand Rothschild for £56,000. The current price of wheat was a little under 3s. 4d. per bushel. Thus the bushel of wheat bore an exchange ratio of $\frac{1}{1039}$th to the egg and of $\frac{1}{336,000}$th to the postage-stamps. This was expressed by the sum of £173 : 5s. as the price respectively of the egg and of 1039 bushels of wheat, and of £56,000 as the price of the stamps and 336,000 bushels. On the other hand the value of these several commodities to their respective buyers can only be gauged by the worth which each attached to his purchase for its usefulness in satisfying his needs or in giving him personal gratification. The egg would bring distinction to its possessor as a rarity, would enable him to please friends and others by its exhibition, or in the case of the Fur Store may have served as a business advertisement. The purchaser of the postage-stamps would be influenced also by mixed motives; but the wheat could be used only for the support of human life, or as seed.

Natural price and market price.

We must regard price in two distinct aspects, the natural and the market price. The former can only be represented by the amount of human labour embodied in the commodities exchanged. But human labour cannot be subdivided, assayed and stamped, and the market price, expressed in coin, is that with which we propose to deal.

The market price considered.

The market price is one of constant fluctuation caused by the struggle of individuals to obtain exclusive use of a commodity, either as a means for personal gratification or for diverting to their own pockets by its resale the largest possible share of the national wealth. Hence the tricks of the market to which the struggle leads. To create a fictitious scarcity or to simulate an active demand is the object of speculators or dealers for whom the market is a sphere of operation. Custom, resting perhaps on the universal desire of men to gain similar ends, condones practices which would be denounced outside of the market as unscrupulous, immoral, and unpatriotic. Certain limitations are understood, but within them much may be done that would not be tolerated in the ordinary relations of life. To the individual operating in the market, supply and demand are the regulators of price. To the consumer, which means to the world at large, supply and demand occupy a position exactly the reverse. They are regulated by price, which brings them to a final equilibrium. A high price stimulates supply and decreases demand. A low price stimulates demand and decreases supply. The point of equilibrium will be the cost at which the commodity can be produced at the particular time. Watches, for example, cost much more when made by hand than when made by machinery, but the latter is the cost to which all must conform or their manufacture cease. The madder plant once so largely cultivated as a dye and now superseded by aniline products, the once famed hand-made muslins of India, and numerous other instances might be cited of products losing their hold on the market by cheaper modes of production, or by having others replace them.

The costs of production. The costs of production are said, in a general sense, to consist of wages, capital, and profit. But this throws us back on another question, what regulates the cost of these elements of production in their turn? Wages represent present labour, and capital represents past labour. Wages must afford a proper subsistence to the labourer. They must enable him to pay taxes and similar charges, as well as make provision for old age or casual need. Capital must return to its owner a proper subsistence, having due regard to the risks and anxieties of his position, and a surplus that will enable him to meet the rent, taxes, and other charges which fall to his share. It must also provide him with the means of increasing his operations if production is not to stand still. The simpler way, therefore, is to consider labour, representing both wages and capital, as the only element in production. The new product must have an exchangeable value equivalent to the labour, in various forms, which it embodies and to the liabilities which that labour has to meet.

<small>Labour power and wages.</small>

Human labour power is not itself a commodity, nor is it subject to the same conditions. Price does not in the same way regulate supply and demand nor reduce them to an equilibrium. On the contrary, we know from experience that in countries where the standard of life is low and the staple of life cheap, population will increase with great rapidity even when the wages of labour scarcely permit human existence. Ireland in the potato era, and the rice-eating countries of the East in the present day, are cases in point. The real and only permanent ruler of wages is the standard of life for the worker and the price of the commodities by which that standard can be met. In the term worker we include all who are engaged directly or indirectly in production and whether by mental or manual labour. A different standard of life will, in the nature of things, be necessary for different classes of work and for the people by whom each class of work is done. In no case, however, should the standard be lower than that which is necessary to satisfy man not only as an animal but an intellectual being. This is the true living wage. The tendency is ever to fall below that point. The main function of trades and other unions is to counteract this tendency, but their separate spheres are limited, and there is always the mass of unorganised unemployed to be brought into the field against them. A solidarity of wage dependents of every kind would be the most efficient counteractor, but education must be widely diffused before the class feeling, which is one of the greatest impediments, can be overcome.

The living wage.

Education not only raises the standard of human life but impels to resistance if wages fall below the point which that standard dictates. Under present conditions the capitalist may decline to enter upon an undertaking when he does not see in it a sufficiently large margin. It is not worth his while, a phrase which the wage dependent cannot use. Herein lies the whole difference between them. To popular education we must look to raise the standard of life and afterwards to enlist public sympathy in every struggle to maintain it. When the wage dependent is in addition an element of weight in the political world, struggles will not be lightly provoked. The best of the employers will also desire to see their people in comfort and themselves saved from being forced by unscrupulous competition to reduce them below that state. A living wage in its higher sense is the lowest reward to which the wage dependent should be entitled, and no industry will be healthy or desirable in which the payment of this wage cannot be met as a first charge upon the new commodity when it is produced.

There are few commodities in these days of machinery in which the wages do not, after all, form a comparatively small proportion of the price at which the commodities are sold. It is computed that any ordinary workman in a factory can

Respective positions of capital and labour in production.

produce with much less than four hours' daily labour all that is required for the proper support of an ordinary family. We know that eight hours are the least that are given, and that in some industries the hours exceed ten. The surplus hours are the source from which come the various charges for rent, taxes, and extraneous outlay borne by the wage dependent. From them also must come the return of his capital to the owner, his remuneration, the various charges to be borne by him, and provision for increased production in the following year. The heavier therefore the rent, royalties, taxes, and other compulsory charges which the capitalist has to meet, the less will remain for his remuneration, and the less will be his inducement to enter upon an undertaking. The only way in which he can make good the deficiency is by reducing the share of the wage worker on the new product which they have jointly created. He must either pay less in wages or get a greater number of hours' work in return. He might reduce his own personal expenditure, but would probably find, in many cases, that the amount so saved is much too small to make good the deficiency. Political economy, looking to the national welfare as its first consideration, will hold that the payment of a living wage must be a first charge upon the new product. The surplus will be the source to which the capitalist must look, and is the only portion upon which taxation can be properly levied except in times of great national need.

If it be found that any particular industry

Industries unable to pay a living wage are public injuries.

cannot be undertaken or cannot be continued on these terms, the burden should be removed from the shoulders of the capitalist and the industry assumed, if practicable, by the State. If that be not practicable, far better abandon it altogether as a public nuisance and a national wrong. Abandoned also, as a gross national wrong, should all industries be that can only exist by substituting for home labour the labour of inferior races, who are sure to sap the national life and to prove a broken reed when a time of emergency comes. In a nation governing itself on these principles, there would probably be fewer buyers of Auk's eggs or postage-stamp collections at fabulous prices, but there would be no homes without bread, and the grower of the wheat would have a larger and better market at his door.

With industry, as with an army and every other human pursuit requiring skill, science, and study to produce satisfactory results, the brain workers must lead. Without them the manual workers become a disorganised and an aimless mass. To assert that leaders are unnecessary is childish and opposed to experience and common sense. The assertion that the State can be trusted to provide such leaders must be received with the limitation that the undertaking will admit of unreserved publicity and regularity of routine in management. There are many such undertakings now in the hands of companies which could be so dealt with—the railways, tramways, water works, docks, gas works, and others in which the wage workers are too often exploited by long hours or poor

Industrial leaders must be paid suitably but kept in check.

pay, to the injury of the nation of which they form part. The story has been told of a great match manufacturer who gave official evidence as to the impossibility of raising the wretched pittance of the workers without ruin to the trade, but who died shortly after and left nearly £200,000 to be divided among his heirs. These are the abuses of capital which call for remedy. Safeguards against abuse are taken when we deal with the leaders of armies, of ministries, and of men in public affairs. With the leaders of industry they are even more needful.

<small>Effect of abundance or scarcity of the precious metals on price.</small>

The precious metals when coined are used to express price. Their own price is nominally unalterable, but nominally alone. Any one may take a certain amount of gold to the mint and will in return receive a fixed amount in coin. The varying amount of other commodities which he can afterwards obtain with the coin is the form in which fluctuations in the price of gold are exhibited. If gold abounds, its own quoted price will remain unaltered but quotations for other commodities will rise. If gold is scarce, then quotations will fall. In the former case the gold is said to be depreciated because it commands less of other commodities in exchange. In the latter case the gold is said to be appreciated because it commands more of other commodities in exchange. When the currency, be it gold or silver, is depreciated and prices rise, the debtor class, always the most numerous in the active wage-paying world, benefits in proportion. When the currency is appreciated the creditor class gains, and with it all who have fixed incomes of any kind. In the debtor class the consequence of currency appreciation is, in innumerable cases, disastrous. All who have fixed obligations, rents or interest to pay, mortgages to meet, or other liabilities calculated on the old ratio of commodities to coin, find their burden enormously increased. They must produce so much the more to get the same amount of coin. Their power of employing others begins to fail and depression spreads in widening circles. The ranks of the unemployed swell and numbers may be reduced to great straits. Yet those fortunate enough to be employed find that their money goes further, and all who have fixed incomes benefit in a similar way. Traders fail, but new men beginning under the new conditions take their place. Some capitalists may suffer or be even ruined by depreciation in property, but many capitalists will be greatly benefited by a fall in prices which makes their securities command commodities to perhaps double their original extent. The combined effect may thus be made, by partial statistics, to show a considerable increase of wealth while the vitality of the nation is being actually undermined.

As a matter of fact, comparative statistics seldom cover the whole field and are delusive unless they do. Common sense and experience are far from infallible guides, but it is difficult to avoid concluding that the recent demonetisation of silver on so great a scale is the chief cause of the universal reduction in the price of commodities which has shaken the social as well as industrial world, and of which the political results have yet

The demonetisation of silver.

to be seen. Not only the silver coin, but the credit built upon it, has been suddenly withdrawn, while obligations calculated on the old basis were left intact. That the silver, from its abundance, might drive out gold to a great extent and render transactions more difficult with countries admitting only gold as current coin is clear. That this would be an injury so serious as the dislocation of society in every direction, the misery, and the terrible cares and anxieties brought upon all classes by so great a derangement of prices, few who regard the case dispassionately will believe. The worst feature is that the false step once taken cannot be easily retraced. New interests are created and the currency controversy seems a mere sordid conflict of interests, as there is no clear central moral principle on which could be rallied the great quiet class whose action is always decisive.

Nor can any description of the results of appreciation or depreciation in currency apply equally to all nations. Much depends upon the social and industrial condition of each at the time. Take, for illustration, the nations of the East, and certain islands in the Pacific whose currency is the silver rupee or silver dollar. The depreciation of their currency stimulates exports largely, because the importing merchant finds it better to remit produce, even at considerable loss, than to remit the rupee or dollar to be sold at a greater loss as bullion. He recoups himself by adding a high exchange to the cost of his imported goods which he sells for the currency of the

<small>Varying effects of appreciation or depreciation of currency in different countries.</small>

country. The buyer of those goods may be in receipt of regular income in rupees or dollars and a considerable loser by the higher price, but the grower of the exportable produce can well afford to lose on the small quantity of imported goods which he buys while receiving so much higher a price for all the produce which he sells. The grower may be the native himself or he may be an employer of native labour, as with tea, coffee, or wheat in India, or coffee and copra in other places. The wages which the employer pays are little if at all increased, because the standard of life is poor, the labourers probably grow all their own food, and their wants otherwise are few. The labourer often grows enough for his own wants and works for others only when he has no surplus with which to buy the few imported articles he may desire. The land is widely distributed and the people often work only for the wretched additions which they consider luxuries in their miserable existence. They get a larger number of coins for the produce which they sell. They see that they have to pay a larger number for the proportion which they spend in imported goods. They limit their purchases accordingly, but the problem is altogether beyond them, and on the whole they are, and have reason to be, satisfied with the higher prices which their produce brings.

The condition of the masses of people in more advanced communities whose standard of life is higher, whose wants are more numerous, and who, above all, must obtain hard cash at every step they

Effect on communities with large wage dependent classes.

take, is widely different. They have no land upon which to put up a shelter; none from which they can draw the least aid in food. They have nothing to sell but their labour power, and they must take that to a glutted market in which the number of competitors for food and shelter is being rapidly increased by the low prices of products of every kind. The farmer finds himself confronted with produce brought from countries favoured either by nature for the easy production of certain articles, as wheat, or favoured by a superabundance of cheap land, as with dairy produce and fresh meat. The nation will not consent to a policy that would protect the growers' market, because the landlord and not the cultivator would reap the benefit. Such conditions are very different to those which confront the student of currency problems in India, in China, or in any other of the countries where the occupancy of the land is widely diffused, and where the standard of living is raised little above the necessaries of animal existence for the great mass of the nation.

At the root of the questions connected with price lies the necessity of making a living wage the first charge on every product. To do this, a nation must, to a commanding degree, be self-contained, placing its chief reliance on its own people as consumers as well as producers, on its own agriculture, its own manufactures, and its own capital. This must not be done after the Chinese fashion where the Mandarin is everything and the worker of no account. The

A living wage the first claim on all production.

whole population must be educated, free, and prosperous to make a sound, strong, and healthy nation. Foreign commerce is a splendid addition to the home trade, but a most unsafe reliance. If in order to obtain foreign commerce low wages and a low standard of life are necessary, if it is necessary to offer in sacrifice any class or section of our own people, the commerce is being too dearly bought and can only become destructive to the nation.

CHAPTER VIII

EXCHANGE

THE basis of all exchange is the aim to secure, by a certain amount of labour, some commodity which would cost a greater amount of labour if made on the spot instead of being obtained by exchange. The advantage in such transactions is mutual, and the greater their number and amount the greater will be the wealth of the nation. *Mutual benefit in exchange.*

The trade resulting from these exchanges may be domestic or foreign. The domestic trade has its origin in the varying natural *Domestic and foreign trade.*

facilities of various parts of the same country. The extent of this trade depends on the consuming power of the people, which depends, in its turn, on the distribution among them in fair proportions of the commodities produced with their labour. On the domestic trade, fostered by concurrent progress in the development of agriculture, mines, manufactures, and of the resources from the coasts and ocean, the true greatness of a nation depends.

Functions of a foreign trade. Among a people industrious and aided by machinery, a large surplus will be produced beyond their needs for ordinary consumption. This surplus may be appropriated to exchange for luxuries which a foreign country only can produce. Herein lies the basis of foreign trade. To it may be attached the importation of raw material for manufactures of various kinds. So far as the commodities thus manufactured are used in the importing country the trade is sound and good. When they are manufactured for export to a foreign market they may bring great wealth to particular individuals, but to the nation they are precarious and if too great in proportion to domestic trade are a source of danger and decay. Under such conditions the greatest luxury and display may be seen, but many of the people will be borne down by the necessity of competing with lower nations in the foreign markets on which this species of commerce depends.

In colonies having huge areas of natural grass as in Australia, or capable of being easily grassed by cultivation as in New Export trade in colonies.

Zealand, the staple products are of such character and extent as to render an active export trade indispensable. The domestic market is too small to absorb such products, but the first care of the colonists is to aim at its extension by encouraging woollen factories and similar industries for the consumption at home, as soon as possible, of the products for which a market can only in the first instance be found abroad.

Imports exceeding exports. The foreign trade consists of imports and exports, and in every progressive young, country or wealthy old country the imports must exceed the exports. The excess will represent imports to be used as capital, but for which there can be no corresponding export till the fruits of the expenditure are gathered. It will represent also the profit on exports, the sale of ships, and other earnings which do not appear in the Statistical Custom-House Returns. The surplus of imports beyond exports may become excessive, in which case there is ground for careful investigation. The excess may be caused by over-speculation, or it may be from the export of debentures by the Government or other public bodies, an export more or less beneficial or more or less injurious according to the purposes to which the responding imports are to be applied. In an older country there is always a large amount of annual interest to be received from its foreign investments, and a large return probably from its carrying trade, or tourist expenditure, or other sources not figuring in the Customs Statistical Returns. On the whole, when the imports—in a new country especially—

exceed the exports in a moderate and steady proportion, the excess may be regarded as indicating prosperity.

<small>Exports exceeding imports.</small>

On the other hand, wherever in a country, old or new, the exports persistently exceed the imports, the case calls for prompt and searching inquiry. Either the exports are selling at a loss or there is a great drain upon them for the payment of interest on debts, or meeting the expenditure of absentees, or, it may be, for paying debts public or private. In the last case a great good is of course being attained and the seeds of future prosperity and independence are being sown. As in most matters connected with political economy it is impossible to lay down unvarying general rules. Each case requires careful and special investigation.

Here we bring our notes to an end, with the hope that they may carry a certain amount of suggestiveness to the minds of those who read them. We have endeavoured to get near the sources of phenomena of various kinds and to make them as clear as possible. The subject is so complicated, the issues are so vast, that it would be the height of presumption to aim at the propounding of off-hand remedies. They must come gradually, following a public opinion that can only be formed after keen and continued discussion. We must first see established the solidarity of labour—mental as well as manual—in order that the solidarity of selfish personal interests may be overcome. Then we may have a real freedom of contract, and State Socialism as a remedy for existing evils be set entirely

What we may hope in the future.

aside as unnecessary. Then we may see the unemployed disappear and the curse and canker of pauperism eradicated from the nation. With a sound and just system of taxation, with the land occupied by millions where thousands now find a place, with the circulating medium taken from the control of capitalists and opened directly to producers of all kinds, with machinery under proper control and contributing its fair share to the national taxation, with the domestic trade developed among a prosperous people and with foreign commerce holding only a subordinate place, a nation may be really great, really strong, and really independent. Such, let us hope, the colonies of Great Britain, now rapidly growing into kindred nations, will one day become, resting their progress and their happiness on no fanciful basis, accepting the acquisitiveness of man as the foundation of progress, but careful to see that the acquisitiveness is kept within due and reasonable bounds.

No particular form of government can accomplish these ends. In the monarchical countries of Europe, whether free or despotic, we find a uniform shoot coming from a healthy ideal. In republican France it is the same; and this is how Mr. Edward Atkinson speaks of the state of affairs in the republican, rich, and powerful United States of America. Reading a paper in Boston, and therefore speaking deliberately, he said, "We are smothered in the abundance of our own products. We are burdened with an excess of all the necessaries of life. We are furnished with more than adequate means of transportation. Yet want exists

Smothered in the abundance of our own products.

in the midst of plenty." Few will dispute that such a condition of affairs is unnatural. To suppose it incapable of remedy is an insult both to God and man.

<small>General Booth in Sydney.</small>

At Sydney in New South Wales, General Booth of the Salvation Army addressed a crowded meeting in the Town Hall on the 19th November 1895. He spoke strongly of the ubiquity of human misery. " When he came to South Africa, that land of gold and diamonds, he asked his followers have you found any of the miseries which you left behind ? They said that they were there. He asked them did you find any slum life like there was in London ? They said they had found something quite as hideous. . . . In the United States he found misery. The Press told him that 10,000 tramps and homeless men were wandering over the country. There was a mighty army of criminals and lost men and women who were earning their living by trading on the weakness of others. During the winter there were between three and four millions without work. . . . He wanted these new countries to look matters calmly in the face and set themselves to stop the evils which affected the older cities of Europe." Here is eloquent testimony, and it was followed by an eloquent appeal in the name of Christianity—the only creed, we may add, which has ever preached the fatherhood of the one God and the universal brotherhood of man. Many may object to the esthetic side of the Salvation Army, to its ritual and service; but all must gratefully recognise the Catholic spirit of Christianity in its deeds and the noble self-sacrifice with which its beneficent work is done. As Economists we venture to think that vice and crime are infinitely less the cause than the effect of poverty. The Christian and the Economist may well work hand in hand, each in his own way, to aid the common cause and to raise humanity to the higher level which—if we have the faith and the hope of true Christians—we must regard it as destined to attain.

THE END

Printed by R. & R. CLARK, LIMITED, *Edinburgh.*

www.ingramcontent.com/pod-product-compliance
Lightning Source LLC
Chambersburg PA
CBHW031815230426
43669CB00009B/1149